The Only Way Through

A Journey of Loss, Transformation and Oneness

ANGELA CAUGHLIN

bright sky press
HOUSTON, TEXAS

2365 Rice Blvd., Suite 202 Houston, Texas 77005

ISBN 978-1-933979-55-7

10 9 8 7 6 5 4 3 2 1

Library of Congress information on file with publisher.

Edited by Hillary Durgin Harmon
Printed in the United States of America

To my three beautiful children,
Kelly, Melissa, and Tom,
and our loving dog, mandy.

Table of Contents

Foreword

By Cynthia Peacock, MD

Loss comes in many forms, from losing your keys to losing a loved one. The loss of keys probably is dealt with immediately, has no lasting effects on the human soul, and life goes on. Getting over the loss of a loved one can take forever, especially if not dealt with psychologically, and it can leave emotional scars. As a physician, I see the most serious forms of loss. It could be a patient dealing with the loss of a family member, overcome by grief. Or, a mother with her newborn baby who has just learned that her child will have significant intellectual and physical impairments; she is overcome with anguish because she realizes her child's full potential will never be realized.

How do I treat loss? Like a disease? Give medication and hope for the best? Sometimes the medication works and numbs the mind, giving it time to heal, consequently enabling the person to postpone dealing with the loss to a future time when they might have better coping skills or support systems. Several times I have heard from patients, "Why did God do this to me?" I suggest they seek help with their pastor, priest, rabbi, or imam with the hope they will explain that these are not God's choices, but that his lessons are there to help them through their grief. Sometimes I refer patients to support groups that deal with loss. Many times I am left wondering how to heal something that I can't see on an X-ray, or feel with my own hands.

Often the experience of suffering a serious loss is not dealt with effectively, and the person becomes tormented by anger and guilt and retreats into isolation. I always fumble for the right words, gestures, or type of guidance I should give. There is never enough time in the day to give the patient because there are always other patients to see and treat.

In 2006, I employed Angela Caughlin to work as a social worker in my clinic. Little did I know at the time that she would be the one who could answer the very question, how can a person effectively deal with a loss? Angela has explored and researched the very valuable tool of writing it down and committing it to a journal. With the template she has developed, the person who is experiencing a loss can be guided through journaling to calmer seas. My copy of her book has been loaned out several times and now is dog eared and weathered. Each time it has come back, the recipient has returned it with a smile and hug for me.

I believe that because of Angela's life experiences and her work with families who have lost a child, the stage was set for her to write this book. Angela has found a method that almost any person can use. The book tells a story that resonates with most people who read it, and it guides them to express their feelings by writing them down. Once again, the pen is mightier than the sword, or, in my case, a pill. Now, I start out with the phrase, "I have this book ..."

I hope that you too find calmer waters as you read Angela's book and use it as a guide.

Cynthia L. Peacock, MD, is the program director of the Combined Medicine-Pediatrics Program at Baylor College of Medicine in Houston

The Mountain

The Garden of Eden

SOMETIMES IN THE MIDST OF AN ORDINARY LIFE SOMETHING EXTRAORDINARY OCCURS.

My name is Angela. I was a wife and a mother, with children who were still young, when my husband, whom I cared for more than anything else in the world, died. His death was tragic and devastating, thrusting me out of what had been my ordinary existence. Yet people die everyday. The extraordinary manifested in time, as I was able to understand and embrace the riveting journey through grief's spiraling maze, finally learning what this loss had to teach me.

I was born and grew up in Houston, Texas. My family didn't possess great wealth, but we were certainly comfortable. We lived in an old subdivision dotted with three-bedroom, two-bathroom houses. The afternoons and summers were spent playing in the grassy front yards up and down the street. It was safe to walk home from school, and there were few organized activities. Playing consisted of made-up games, which included neighborhood children of all ages who would show up on the lawn where we were playing. My father was a partner in a law firm, and his career was successful. My mother was a full-time housewife and, like most families, ours included three children. I was the middle child, always playing with my older sister, Mary, or my younger brother, John. The entire scene could have been from the idealized, family sitcom from the fifties *Ozzie and Harriet*.

It was a simpler time then. Drugs, violence, and casual sex were not pressures that my friends and I had to face as we came up through school. I attended parochial schools during my elementary years, and the nuns who were my teachers thoroughly indoctrinated me with their own conservative values and views of the world and God. Consequently, as a child and a young woman, I had no doubt in my mind that I knew what was right and what was wrong. Rarely, if ever, did it occur to me to question my own beliefs and values, or, more accurately, the beliefs and values I'd been taught. It wasn't until after parochial school, when I attended an enormous public high school, that I had any first-hand exposure to the world that existed outside of the privileged enclave in which I'd grown up. I was a protected person, living in a protected world.

Yet even in my world, everything wasn't perfect, of course. This is a true story, after all. Even ordinary people have problems, and families that seem blessed and privileged on the surface have their own secret struggles. My mother wrestled with a drinking problem that eventually destroyed her health and killed her. I never knew what drove her to drink. She never talked much when she drank or got angry; she would just get quiet and withdrawn. And although my father was brilliant, and I knew he loved us all, he had little skill or ability at showing it. He was a very distant man, quiet and passive. So although I never doubted that my parents loved me, at times their love seemed filtered, or experienced from a distance.

As high school neared its end, I looked forward to college and to getting away from Houston. I wanted a big change. To me, a Catholic girl from a quietly cloistered background, that meant going to Louisiana State University in Baton Rouge, but my father wouldn't hear of it. He'd graduated from The University of Texas at Austin and wanted me to go to UT too. I had a stubborn streak, even then; if he wouldn't let me go to LSU, I wasn't going to go to his choice either. I ended up going to North Texas State University in Denton, a small town near Dallas, just to spite him, and ended up spiting myself. I hated it there, and after one year, transferred to Sam Houston State University in Huntsville, another small town. My academic ambitions were moderate. I expected, by the end of college, to fall in love and marry and stay at home and have children. That was my American dream. It was the life my mother and her friends lived, and I saw no reason why it shouldn't be my life, too.

When college ended, the dream seemed nowhere in sight. I'd dated in college, but had never been tempted to get seriously involved with anyone. Yet life's day-to-day responsibilities don't wait for dreams to come true. So after college, I moved back to Houston, found a job teaching school, and shared an apartment with three other girls.

Things that seem like coincidence have so often changed my life; people met by chance, or opportunities taken, or missed. During the spring, after I'd moved back to Houston, I was dating a boy named Jim. One of his friends, Tom Caughlin, was dating one of my roommates. One day Tom stopped by the apartment, looking for her. She was gone; I was the only one there. On a whim, maybe, I'm not sure why he did it, Tom suggested we drive down to Galveston for the day.

I don't know why I agreed. After all, I was dating one of his best friends, and Tom had a reputation of being somewhat of a ladies' man. He was three years older than I was, which at that age seemed like a lot. I agreed, though. I know now it was one of those things that is destined to happen in a person's life.

It was an incredibly beautiful day, the kind that's made to be part of a memory. The sun was shining brightly, but the weather hadn't turned hot yet. Tom had a shiny, little green sports car with two seats. We drove with the top down, letting the wind whip through our hair.

When we reached Galveston, we walked on the beach for hours, just talking. I don't remember what we talked about. The words weren't important. It was the way we talked that startled us both. The conversation never struggled. There was never any loss for words, or any strain. We could talk about anything, with no awkwardness at all. Ironically, I have to struggle now to find words to convey what was so free and easy then. Something passed between us that day, beyond words. Maybe our souls themselves touched. All I know is that we were able to communicate effortlessly and completely, and it was intoxicating.

Tom surprised me by kissing me. It was one of the

turning points in my life. I knew, after that kiss, that there was no going back to my life before. Tom felt it too. Tom looked a little shaken, and told me, "You'd better talk to Jim. We both know what's happening here." And he was right. I did know.

We never looked back. By summer, we'd decided to marry. Fortunately, almost from the moment they'd met him, both of my parents grew quickly to adore Tom. Even so, they were surprised by the suddenness of our decision. My mother, in particular, tried to test the seriousness of my resolve. She knew I'd always wanted to go to Europe, so she told me, "We'll either send you to Europe, or we'll do a wedding." Without hesitating I told her, "I'm getting married." And in October, just six months after that day when Tom and I had walked on the beach in Galveston, we did.

Looking back, those early years of our marriage seemed so easy, so carefree. I guess in a way it was like the calm, sunny day before an unsuspected storm. Tom didn't have a very serious disposition. He had lots of friends, and he liked to have fun. We were a very social couple. We went out frequently with lots of other couples, and we did lots of things with my parents as well; they loved Tom. For one thing, Tom was very handy and capable, and my father was not. Tom was an only child, and his father had died when he was twelve, so Tom had needed to become the man of his mother's household. Tom could fix anything, and my Dad, who couldn't, was very impressed. He was always happy for Tom's help.

Probably the biggest reason we did so much with my parents, though, was because my father had a boat. Tom loved boats and loved being on the water. In fact, Tom's love of boats caused the first big argument between us after we married. Tom really wanted a boat of his own. One day, he told me he'd figured out that if we sold my car, we could afford to buy a boat that he'd found. I loved my car. It was a graduation present that my father had bought me; but I was young, and just married, and in love, and it didn't occur to me, when he proposed the idea, to question my husband's judgment. It didn't take being without a car for very long, though, before I did start to question it. It seems funny looking back on it now, but at the time, I was furious when it dawned on me too late that I was stuck without any transportation. I certainly couldn't get to where I needed to go in the boat.

Tom worked for an airline, in general sales, and his job required that we move frequently. We moved from Houston to Shreveport, Louisiana, not long after we were married, and then nine months later moved to Dallas. It was while we were in Dallas that Kelly, our first child, was born. Tom and I both knew, before we married, that we wanted children. We differed on the details, though. I wanted four or five children and wanted to start our family right away. To Tom, who'd been an only child, the thought of that many children seemed overwhelming. He wanted no more than two, and wasn't in a hurry for them either. The timing, at least, was a disagreement I won. Tom couldn't believe it when I told him I was pregnant. After all, I was taking the pill. I forgot to tell him that I'd stopped because they made me nauseous. When I did tell him, he said that it was unimportant. He was thrilled once he started thinking about the reality of becoming a father. Tom was good that way. If something upset him, he'd definitely let me know; but he knew how to blow off steam, and then it would be over, as if it had never happened. Tom taught me that skill. He could accept anything and just move on. Almost anything, that is.

It seemed we'd hardly settled in Dallas before we moved again, this time to Denver. Every place we moved, we made new friends because Tom's easy, happy-go-lucky manner just attracted people. But the constant upheaval was wearing. I missed having stability in our lives, and I missed my parents. When, a year after we'd moved to Denver, Tom was transferred back to Houston, he decided it was time to make a jump. He left the airline and took a job with a stock brokerage firm in Houston. It was a kind of work he knew nothing about, but Tom always believed he could master anything if he tried hard enough. So we came back to the city where I'd grown up, the city where we'd met and married, excited about creating a new home for ourselves. It was during that year, after moving back to Houston, that my mother died. Even though she had stopped drinking, it had destroyed her health. It was an enormous sadness that Tom and I grieved over together.

For the first two years, money was tight, and I had to teach school to help support our family. Then Tom's career began to take off. Because of his easygoing manner, he attracted clients as readily as he attracted friends. Before long, Tom rose to become a vice president in his firm.

With Tom's success, I was able to quit working. We wanted more children, but it took more than six years of trying after Kelly was born before I became pregnant with Melissa, our second child. The next shock wave hit us the year after Melissa was born, when we had the devastating news that my father had cancer. He did not live long after his diagnosis. Again, Tom and I felt bound together as the pangs of grief washed over us.

Four years after Melissa's birth, I became pregnant again and had a miscarriage. The miscarriage led to many discussions of whether to try again to have a third child. In the midst of these great talks, I became pregnant with our son, Tom Jr. Tom was ecstatic over having a son. I was becoming aware of the circle of life that connects birth and death.

Tom's successful career brought many material changes to our lifestyle. We bought a big, new home close to downtown, in the kind of old-fashioned neighborhood where your neighbors quickly become your best friends. We bought vacation homes on a lake north of Houston and on the bay down in Galveston, both on the water, which we loved so much. In every area of our lives, it was as though all of our dreams were finally coming true. Or so we thought.

Facing the Bear

IT STARTED WITH SUCH A LITTLE THING. A COUGH. EVERYONE GETS A COUGH NOW AND THEN. IT'S NOT SOMETHING YOU EXPECT WILL KILL YOU.

Tom thought it was just a cold. He was always healthy and active, so he didn't let it slow him down, even when it didn't go away after a couple of weeks. We'd planned to attend a big weekend at a friend's lake house with several other couples, and we wouldn't have dreamed of missing it. The kids and I stayed with the other wives and children at the lake house, while Tom and the men flew down to a ranch in south Texas to hunt.

When they returned, Tom pulled me aside. I could tell from the expression on his face that something was wrong.

"I don't know what's wrong with me," he told me. "I couldn't keep up with the others. I felt exhausted, and my legs were so weak. I must be getting sick. Something more than just a cold."

Tom thought maybe he had a mild touch of the flu. When we got back to town, he went to see a friend who was an internist. As his friend, the internist knew how healthy Tom was. He agreed it was probably just a touch of the flu, and added that possibly it had caused a small infection in Tom's lungs. He prescribed some antibiotics and assured Tom they'd get him back on his feet in no time. Two weeks later, after no improvement, Tom was back in the doctor's office.

This time the doctor ordered a chest X-ray. He called Tom with the results. The X-ray, he told him, showed the presence of a mass in Tom's chest, between his lungs.

I felt shock and terror run through me at the mention of the word "mass." I was raised a Catholic. To me, Mass had always symbolized peace and hope. A time to try and feel the presence of the God I'd always been told was out there somewhere. I never expected that word to take on such a different significance.

Tom had to go into the hospital to have a biopsy done. He was still sedated from the anesthesia when the doctor came out to where I was waiting with Thelma, Tom's mother.

From the expression on his face, I knew things did not look good. "What is it?" I asked him. He said it was a tumor on Tom's lungs and that it was malignant. The next words from my lips were, "How long does Tom have to live?" Maybe I already knew the answer to that question, from the look I could read on doctor's face. "A few weeks, maybe a few months." Thelma grabbed my arm and swayed. I wasn't much stronger as I tried to steady her and guide her to the nearest chair in the waiting area, hoping she wouldn't collapse.

My senses couldn't take in what was happening around me. I just kept thinking, "I've got to get out of here." There was no reason to stay; Tom was still sedated and wouldn't be moved from the recovery room for several more hours. Thelma was stunned. She couldn't talk; she could barely function at all. I had to lead her, the blind leading the blind, but somehow we made it to my car. My thoughts were racing. I wondered if I would ever breathe or think normally again. My body felt like it was moving in slow motion.

I drove around for a while, aimlessly. I remember thinking, finally, that I needed to stop somewhere.

I didn't know where I was going or what I was doing. I don't know how I'd managed not to wreck the car. I pulled into the parking lot of a McDonald's restaurant, and we just sat there, not speaking. We were in shock. There were no words for what we were feeling.

After a couple of hours, we returned to the hospital. Tom was in his room and was now awake. I tried to appear normal as I walked into his room. Thelma had composed herself as well. The doctor had already talked to him, and Tom knew he had cancer. He didn't know how bad it was, though. The doctor hadn't told him what he'd told me. I didn't volunteer any more information because until we had the test results, we didn't know the scope of what we were dealing with. I also knew we were all too fragile to handle any more news at that moment. Just comprehending that he had cancer was enough for all of us.

A few days later, after he'd gotten out of the hospital, Tom went to get a full report from the doctor on the results of the biopsy. He went straight from work, without me. By then I'd started telling myself that maybe the doctor had been mistaken, that maybe things weren't as bad as he'd initially thought. My hopes dissolved when Tom walked in the door. He ripped off his tie as he walked down the hall and burst into tears.

I had never seen Tom cry before. I followed him down the hallway and felt like I was chasing him. It was terrible, and terrifying. I started crying too.

"I'm going to die," he said. We held each other and cried until we were both cried out. After a while, he said, "I'm going to beat this. I have too much to live for." That was Tom. Like anyone, he could be knocked down, but you couldn't keep him down for long.

Kelly, our oldest daughter, had a basketball game that night. It was the last game of the season. I didn't want to go; I didn't want to be around people, to see everyone else living normal lives when ours had just been shattered, but Tom insisted. He was determined to pull us back into normalcy. It was a strain, a terrible effort, pretending to look normal, but I'm glad we went. It was the last time Tom ever saw Kelly play basketball.

It's so hard for a person to accept that they're going to die. Tom couldn't do it. Until the very end, when it was no longer possible to deny, he refused to believe it. Partly, I'm sure it was because he was afraid. But more than fear, I think he felt shame and guilt. Tom had always told me, from the time we'd first known we'd spend our lives together, that he'd always be there for me and take care of me, and I wouldn't have to worry about anything.

I treasured this wonderful part of our relationship, knowing that my life and my cares were in Tom's hands. I let myself depend on him; I welcomed it, and he knew it. And now, he was faced with the fact that he'd no longer be there, that he'd be unable to keep his promise to me. It tormented him. He was afraid of what might happen to our children and me if he wasn't there to take care of us himself. Yet it was totally out of his control.

The reality was more than either of us could accept for long. Denial can be a strong coping mechanism. We told ourselves that maybe the doctor was wrong, that perhaps Tom's chances weren't as bleak as the doctor was telling us. A childhood friend of Tom's named Jack, who was now a doctor himself, offered to take Tom's slides and test results to other specialists to get a second opinion. Maybe the specialists would see something that Tom's doctor had missed or misinterpreted.

What Jack found out didn't give us any new hope. Tom had adenocarcinoma, a form of lung cancer. Only about 1 percent of people afflicted with it survived, and Tom's had metastasized already. It had spread throughout his body, so surgical removal of the cancer was not an option.

"What should I do?" I asked Jack. "What can I do for Tom?"

"If there's anything you've been putting off, a trip you want to take, do it now," he said. "It's difficult to predict how quickly this could go."

It's hard to watch a strong man become weak. Tom had always been strong, not just physically, but emotionally, too. His father had died when Tom, an only child, was just twelve. Despite his young age, he'd stepped up and become the man of the family by providing his mother emotional support, as well as by taking care of whatever needed to be done around their home. The all-too-familiar journey resonated in his mind.

From having grown up with that sense of responsibility for someone else, Tom had developed an incredibly strong work ethic. He hated being around people who were lazy or complainers. Even when he was relaxing, he wanted to be working on something, some project he'd think up.

Even as he became weaker and weaker from the cancer, even when he was far too weak to really do any work at the office, his work ethic didn't change. He was determined to go into work every day. It became an ordeal for everyone around him. Every day, almost all day long, he coughed. It was a horrible, wrenching-sounding cough, the sound of someone struggling just to breath. Sometimes his secretary would call me from work, almost in tears from listening to him sitting in his office and coughing, and beg me to come get him and take him home. His lungs were so damaged that I'd have to pound his back frequently with a cupped hand, a suggested treatment called "back clapping," to try and loosen the congestion in his lungs and help him cough up the phlegm and fluid that were filling them. Sometimes Tom Jr., almost a year then, would be playing cars at the foot of the bed as I was clapping Tom's back. As I looked at young Tom, it felt surreal that I was trying to help his father survive as this child was quietly playing at the foot of our bed. I had to try to stay positive for my family as I constantly fought my feelings of sadness and fear. I thought about how, in the space of a few months, our life had changed so drastically. This was not the way it was supposed to be.

Still, Tom wanted to go to work. He hated that people pitied him or felt sorry for him because he was sick. It made him even more determined to show that it wasn't going to stop him. Trying to navigate this illness with some sense of dignity was supremely important to him. Even as he was obviously weakening, Tom continued to insist that he was going to get better, that he wasn't going to die.

In reality, only a miracle could have saved him. His cancer was so widespread, and so serious, that it was virtually untreatable. We knew, from what Tom's doctor and Jack had told us initially, that surgery wasn't an option. The doctors also told him that chemotherapy would only increase his likelihood of survival by 1 percent. At that time, the chemo treatment was so brutal that, for the time he had left, his quality of life would have been seriously impaired. Tom refused chemotherapy, but he did take radiation treatments to try to kill the cancers that were attacking his body. Those treatments alone, though, were a mere thread to hang our hopes on.

For a short time after he was first diagnosed, Tom went to see a counselor. The doctors who were treating him recommended it. They thought that Tom needed to get help understanding and accepting what was happening to him. He only went to see the counselor a few times, though. Tom told me, "All he wants me to do is accept that I'm going to die. I'm not going to do that. I'm not going to accept it. I'm not going to die!"

There was another counselor who did help Tom some, though. Her name was Alice, and she was a nun who worked as a counselor at the M. D. Anderson Cancer Center in Houston. Alice was a virtual institution at

M. D. Anderson. She was short and motherly, with beautiful gray hair, sparking blue eyes, and a smile that lit up the room. Love radiated from her face and body. She loved angels, and I always thought, like others, that she must somehow get insight from them. Alice lived in an apartment not far from where we lived. At least one night every week, she'd stop by our house after she got off work to see how Tom was doing. He could confide his fears to her. He could tell her the things he couldn't or didn't want to talk about with me. In fact, he could tell Alice anything.

Tom's strength declined quickly, and he was faced with more and more things he could no longer do. He wanted so badly, that last autumn that he was alive, to go hunting with his friends. Tom had always loved the outdoors, and he had loved fishing and hunting. But he just couldn't keep up with his friends anymore. He was too weak.

To try and deal with my own stress, I started taking long walks around the neighborhood. Soon Tom began joining me on my walks, but after a time, he couldn't even keep up on those. This was especially upsetting for him. For a man like Tom, a walk around the neighborhood seemed so insignificant. He'd never have dreamed it would become a challenge he couldn't meet.

It also upset him to see our roles gradually reverse. He'd always been the one who was the caretaker in the family. As he weakened, though, he sometimes would have to spend long stretches of time in bed, and he needed me to care for him. He could no longer be the one who took care of the children and me. More and more frequently, he lacked the strength to even take care of himself. This was as terrifying to him as the cancer—the loss of control over everything around him.

Still, he denied he was dying. For a while we even went shopping for a new house. After Tom Jr.'s birth, just six months before his father was diagnosed with cancer, our house had seemed too small for our growing family. Ignoring the fact that our family could possibly change, Tom and I searched for a new home to move to and talked as if we've be spending years together in it.

Tom was diagnosed in October. At first, he got steadily worse, as the doctors had predicted. Then, in December, as Christmas approached, it seemed like Tom's optimism was going to prove to be justified. The doctors told us that the most recent X-rays showed that the big tumor in Tom's chest had shrunk from the radiation treatments. We clung to those words with every shred of hope we could muster. We told ourselves that Tom's faith, his optimism, were justified, that he was going to beat the cancer. The news came in the knick of time, and that helped make our Christmas a time of hope and happiness.

But it was fleeting. In January, Tom started worsening again. A new tumor appeared, this time in his leg. From that point on, it seemed Tom was speeding faster and faster toward his death. Another apparent coincidence happened in January. Our family collie, sandy, became very ill. She was fourteen years old, but the suddenness of her illness took our family by surprise. She died very peacefully, simply walking out in our backyard and quietly hiding in the back part of the garden. We found her behind the bushes, late in the afternoon, after wondering if she had slipped out of the yard. She was too big to bury in the backyard, so Tom had the difficult task of taking her body to the vet. As he left the house with her body, our teary eyes met, and, in unspoken words, we both knew that somehow this event was preparing us for the next, even more difficult part of our path.

A few months after little Tom had been born, and a few months before we learned that big Tom had cancer, I joined a Bible study group at our church. It was not the sort of thing I'd ever done before, but with the birth of our third child, I'd started thinking about how I wanted our family to be. Materially, we had no cares, thanks to Tom's success in his career. We had money, and we enjoyed spending it. In many ways, we weren't unlike my own parents. We owned vacation homes in addition to the house we lived in, which was in a wonderful neighborhood in Houston. We had nice cars and a boat, and we belonged to a country club. But in my family when I was growing up, especially in my teen years, I'd sensed that something was lacking in my parents' lives. My mother must have sensed it, too, because that was when she'd started drinking heavily and had so frequently seemed quietly sad. So when I looked at the families with whom Tom and I were friends and who seemed the happiest, I wanted to know what made them that way. I realized that all of the happiest, closest families we knew seemed to focus not just on material things but also on the spiritual side of life. I decided that would become a bigger part of our lives too. I chose the Bible study group as the way I would start along that path.

Once Tom became sick, I was so glad I'd done that. My parents had both been dead for some years by then. My mother had died when Kelly was just a year old. And my father had died in the year after Melissa was born, just as we were preparing to move into our new home. Neither had lived to see their grandson. Neither was there to give me the comfort and support I needed when Tom became sick. My brother and sister were also living in other cities, making our reliance on and support from friends even more important.

My prayer life started to take on a new dimension. I had the sense that we were being surrounded by exactly the support that we needed. The new friends I'd made in the Bible study group gave me tremendous comfort, on every level. We prayed together, and I could talk to them about what was happening to Tom and to me, about my fears. They were always there with a meal, or helping with the children, when I didn't have the time or strength for anything but Tom.

Another source of support that became essential to me was a wonderful woman who had worked for my grandmother for many years. Her name was Clarice. Clarice had many grandchildren of her own, was a great cook and lots of fun, and we needed some fun! She came and helped more and more as Tom's condition worsened, and as I had to be at the hospital and at doctor appointments. I could always count on Clarice. Throughout Tom's illness, she held my hand and wiped my tears. Her understanding of God and spirituality provided a great sounding board for me, as she helped to steady me on the beginning of this bigger walk.

In the last months, from January until early March when Tom died, he was so sick and weak that he had to spend more and more time in the hospital. He hated being there. It was proof he couldn't ignore that he wasn't beating the cancer. No matter how hard Tom tried, no matter how strongly he willed that he'd survive, death was winning, not Tom. During one of his hospital stays, the vice president of human resources from Tom's brokerage firm came to the hospital to talk to him. He told Tom that he had to stop trying to come to work. He told him that he had to go on disability leave. Tom started crying. He always had been so proud of how he'd supported the children and me, and now this man was telling him that he couldn't do it any more.

Tom believed in God, but his belief, like mine at that time, was not very evolved. He didn't understand why he had to die, and it made him angry. After all, he was only thirty-nine. He had always worked hard and tried to do the right thing. He had a wife and three young children who needed his support. Why did he have to die, he'd ask me, when so many people in the world had choices that were no longer an option to him. As much as we had planned our life, it was now completely out of our control.

I didn't know the answer. I didn't understand either. The

Bible study group had helped strengthen my faith that there was a God, and that there was a heaven that Tom would go to when he died. But they didn't have answers for that kind of question. Who does? Like Tom, I was angry that Tom had to die now, while we were both so young and had so much still ahead of us to live for. Sometimes, when I was alone in my room and trying to pray to God, my anger would overflow, and I'd shout and scream at him instead of praying to him—not that my prayers for help or my anger seemed to make any difference. Inexorably, Tom got weaker and weaker.

Even after the firm's vice president had told Tom to go on disability, for a little while after he got out of the hospital, Tom still tried to go to work. But he had so little strength, and the new tumor made his leg especially weak. One morning, he got up and said he was going to go to work that day. When he tried to get into the shower, though, his leg gave way, and he collapsed. He couldn't get back up, he was too weak even with my help, and I wasn't strong enough to get him up on my own. My husband, my once, so-strong Tom, was lying helpless on the bathroom floor.

It was more than I could stand.

"I can't handle this any more, Tom," I told him with tears

streaming down my face. "I can't do this anymore. You have to go. You have to go into the hospital."

I ran outside and found a thirteen-year-old boy, Mike, the son of one of our neighbors. I grabbed Mike and told him that he would have to help me get Tom up and dressed, and get him into the car. Mike and Tom both had tears in their eyes as Mike put both arms under Tom's big shoulders and lifted him off the bathroom floor. We both supported him as we lifted him into the car. With tears streaming down my cheeks, I was not sure how I was going to drive, and I knew for Tom it was a one-way trip. Two weeks later he was dead.

During those last two weeks, there was an outpouring of kindness and love from everyone who had known Tom. One of Tom's friends who owned a grocery store had special meals prepared for him and delivered to his room every day, so he wouldn't have to eat hospital food. Frequently, Tom was too sick to eat, but his friend kept sending meals anyway, just in case. All of our friends from Houston, and many of Tom's old friends from Port Arthur where he'd grown up, came to the hospital in a constant stream to visit him. They were all coming to say goodbye. Tom's best friend from childhood, Jimmy, never left his side during those last painful days. He would catch a few hours of sleep on one of the couches outside of Tom's room. His presence was steady, and reassuring. He had been Tom's lifelong friend, and he wasn't bailing out because it was tough.

One night, Tom's whole office came as a group. They all stood or sat around his bed, and laughed and told jokes with him. I remember one of them teased Tom, nudging his leg where it lay on the bed under the covers, and said, "Come on Caughlin, enough of this. Get up and get out of bed." Another told him the whole office was missing his dirty jokes, and that his were always the best—or the worst, depending on how you looked at it.

In the last weeks, even before he went into the hospital the final time, Tom knew that he was going to die. One day, not long before he collapsed that morning in our home, he'd insisted I go to his office with him. That wasn't something he'd done before.

"If I don't make it through this," he told me, "you need to know all of these things," and he'd sat me down and explained where all of our financial information and accounts were. He also arranged to sell our vacation house up at Lake Conroe. He wanted that finalized as soon as possible, he said, so the money from the sale would be available for whatever I might need. He teared up many times during that discussion, feeling that despite all of his precise and careful planning, the years to come would be out of his control. It seemed like another small step toward accepting the inevitable path on which we had been placed.

Tom told me that when the end came, if it was time for him to go, he wanted to die; he didn't want to be put on life support. Our friend Jack, the doctor, told me I had to be sure and honor Tom's wishes on that. "Everyone has the right to make that decision for themselves," he said.

During his last days in the hospital, Tom's mother, Thelma, was with him almost constantly, but sometimes, because of the kids, I couldn't be there. Thelma was an energetic, dark-haired woman from Port Arthur. She was an amazing cook, and could hold her own in any poker game in town. She was a survivor in many aspects of her life, and Tom was her world. She had endured the death of Tom's father, and he had been the love of her life. Now she was losing the only other person whom she adored.

Between Jimmy, Thelma, and myself, Tom was never alone. I was beginning to realize how quickly he was going, and I didn't want to leave him with just anyone. He got so scared at the end; he was afraid I wouldn't be there when he died. He'd call me up every day if I hadn't come to the hospital by late morning, and ask me to get a babysitter, and come to be with him. He realized what I didn't. He knew that he didn't have much time, and he wanted me there at the end.

As if gloating at its victory over him, the cancer became visible on Tom's body in the last few days of his life. New tumors appeared all over his chest and arms, right under the surface of his skin. His whole body was being ravaged, and death's approach could no longer be ignored.

Our son, Tom, was a little over a year old, and Melissa was just five, but I brought Kelly, now twelve, to the hospital to tell Tom goodbye. There had been some family friends visiting earlier that night, but when I took Kelly into the room to see her father, it was just the three of us.

Kelly hadn't seen Tom since he'd gone into the hospital that last time. His arms, always so strong and muscular, were now starting to sag, and he could barely lift them. His breath was short, and he gasped when he tried to talk. He kept his smile, as tears seeped out of the corners of his eyes. He looked very different; as the cancer ravaged him, his appearance had really deteriorated. Kelly walked over to his bed and just took his hand and held it. She couldn't speak at all; she just stood there, holding his hand and quietly crying, while Tom told her how much he loved her. They stayed like that for hours. Memories of all the years of Tom coaching her in T-ball, camping with her on Indian Princess trips, and picking her up from summer camp—Kelly so excited to tell us about all she'd done, but at the same time so excited to be coming home—flooded over me. I remember thinking that we take so much for granted in our lives.

I found myself, in those final days, getting angry at the people who were visiting. I looked for things to find fault with, things I felt were wrong or inconsiderate. I'd feel annoyed if visitors brought young children with them, or if I felt they were staying too long and tiring Tom. I was upset by what they all had, and by what I was losing.

Denial can be so strong, even when you know the end is near. At times, I questioned the amounts of morphine the doctors were giving Tom, as if it could matter in his future, when, in reality, there was no more future. On the last day, I knew the end was not far off. Tom was having more and more trouble breathing. By then, he was heavily sedated with morphine because of the pain, and over the final hours, he drifted in and out of sleep. Then suddenly, he was wide awake and looking at me.

"I'm dying," he said. "We all have to go."

I was a mess. I was sitting by his hospital bed, with my arms wrapped tightly around him and my head lying on his chest. I started bawling my eyes out, and telling him, "You can't go," over and over again.

"I have to go," he said. And he told me, "You will never have to worry. You're going to be just fine. And I will never leave you."

And then, as I gently held him, I heard his last breath, and he left us.

In the Valley

Looking at Shadows

THE NURSE WALKED INTO THE ROOM. IT SEEMED AS IF I HAD BEEN HOLDING TOM FOR HOURS, ALTHOUGH IT HAD BEEN ONLY MINUTES. SHE QUIETLY ASKED ME IF I WERE READY TO "LET THEM TAKE HIM." ALL I COULD FEEL WAS ANGER AND IRRITABILITY. I FELT SHE WAS INTRUDING. I ANSWERED HER IN A VERY SURLY TONE, "NO, I AM NOT READY; IN FACT, I MIGHT NOT EVER BE READY. I MIGHT STUFF HIM AND TAKE HIM HOME." I FELT LIKE I HAD LOST ALL CONTROL. A SHOCKED LOOK CAME OVER HER FACE, AND THEN SHE GENTLY SMILED WITH GREAT UNDERSTANDING AND QUIETLY TOLD ME I COULD HAVE AS MUCH TIME AS I NEEDED, AND THEY WOULD CHECK BACK WITH ME. THEY HAD TO DO THE AUTOPSY.

As I held his body I felt crazy, like this scene was not real. Denial and shock engulfed my being. I thought, "How could I possibly let them take his body, this body I had cared for day in and day out for the last six months? He belongs to me!" His body lay limp in my arms. I turned my head and put my ear down on his chest, as if I expected to hear something. There was nothing, no sound. Now, it was over. He had breathed his last breath. I had heard that last breath. I had breathed that last breath with him. No more coughing, no more yucky stuff coming up from his lungs, no more tests, no more fear. The worst had finally happened, and it was really over.

I felt myself being gently ushered into another room. I had no idea how much time had elapsed since Tom had died. Time meant nothing. A priest was there and several close friends. I had stopped crying. I felt nothing, absolutely nothing, total numbness. I heard them talking, but I had no idea what they were saying. I just stared at all of them; what they were saying didn't matter, nothing mattered anymore.

The morning after Tom's death, Alice, the counselor from M. D. Anderson, stopped by the house for coffee. It was nice to see a familiar face who understood how we were feeling. Five-year-old Melissa came bouncing into the breakfast room and sat on Alice's lap. She proceeded to tell us where she had been the night before.

"Last night after I went to sleep, Daddy came and got me. We laughed and played all night! I even sat on his lap, and he tickled me like he used to do. We played 'horsey,' and he bounced me up and down! He showed me all these places he gets to go. When it was morning, he brought me back, but he wanted me to know he was okay, and he didn't want me to worry because I had not gone to the hospital to say goodbye. Daddy is just fine, and having so much fun!"

Alice and I sat there in shock! Melissa was absolutely clear that this had really happened. This was my first realization that Tom was close by and that maybe his last words, "I will never leave you," had more meaning than I had realized.

Watching Tom die, and letting go of everything, suddenly put everything pertaining to life into a different perspective for me. The age-old questions, "Why am I here?" and "What is my purpose?" had been on my mind during the past few months. Tom and I had talked about this just weeks before he died. He questioned why the others got to live, when he had so much to live for, and we knew that death was inevitable.

Over the following weeks and months I was trying to

figure out who I was and grapple with the enormity of what I had lost. It was all I could do to get out of bed, get Kelly and Melissa out the door to school, and stare out the window. My roadmap, which before had always been reliable, was muddled and had been torn apart. It was as if I didn't fit anywhere. I had three children, no husband, and a lot of fear. Did God really know what he was doing? All of the dreams and things I felt that I had been promised, all of the words I had read in the Bible, were they really true? I was questioning everything. I had taught school when Tom and I first married, but knew that a career in teaching could not support my family on a long-term basis. Over the next year, I did not work. I struggled to regain my balance and to try and make sense out of what had happened to me.

I felt obligated to give my children enormous amounts of love; friends can only do so much. But my energy felt drained, and my ability to concentrate was impaired. Sometimes when one of the children would ask me something, I would not even hear. I always felt preoccupied. Later I learned that this was normal grief, but at the time it felt like I was going crazy. I also learned that some people only take a few weeks off from work after a death. Looking back at my own inability to function, I wondered how that could be possible.

I craved things that helped life seem normal again, but I didn't know what normal was anymore. Clarice, who had been a consistent support since Tom's illness began, continued to come and help me with the children. She continued to offer great insights into the spiritual aspect of what was happening to me. I also realized that my own parenting abilities and patience were drained, and my children needed her positive attitude and support. Sometimes when she spent the night, she even let them have ice cream for breakfast. Little treats mean a lot when you are grieving!

Living alone was a big adjustment. I missed Tom every day. I missed his smile, his teasing, and his laughter, which had seemed to fill our home. It seemed so quiet and uneventful without him. I missed him playing with the children, and just having that someone walk in the door and wonder what was for dinner that night. The weekends were by far the hardest, trying to plan things without Tom. Fortunately, the lake house we owned had sold a few days before he died; it had no longer felt fun to go, even though it was surrounded by wonderful memories.

After the sale, I went there to clean it out for its new occupants. The house was nestled in a quiet part of the lake, surrounded by trees. The children had loved to walk in the wooded area near the house on the empty roads that were being laid in the new part of the subdivision. There was one particular part of the road that we called "bunny corner." It was a brushy area that was home to a family of rabbits. Tom and I would take the children in the late afternoon to watch the bunnies at bunny corner.

Kelly loved to water ski. We kept the boat at the boat dock not far from the house. But how do you drive a boat alone with three small children? I no longer had a captain. How would I have managed the upkeep of another house and a boat? The lake house was no longer a fit for our family. At the end, Tom had known this. It had been a wise decision to sell. It was interesting that it had happened just days before he died.

As I cleaned out the rooms in the lake house, the memories came flooding back. I felt Tom's presence in every part of the house. He had built out much of the interior with the help of his friends. It had been the first place we had taken Tom Jr. after he was born. We had caught fireflies at night and fish during the day. Tom had taught both Kelly and Melissa how to bait a hook with those yucky worms. My tears streamed down my face as I packed. How could I be doing this alone? This wasn't the way it was supposed to be. So many dreams shattered.

Shortly before Tom's death, we had planned a trip to Disneyworld and Destin, Florida, with our neighbors, Bobby and Pam, and their children. They were a wonderful family and had children close to the ages our own. One of my biggest first decisions after Tom's death was whether to embark on this trip with them. Tom had died in March, and May was the designated time to leave on the trip. I was tempted to cancel; my energy felt so depleted that I wasn't sure I would be good company for anyone. After much begging from my children, and with loving encouragement from Bobby and Pam, we prepared for the trip. Bobby did all the preparation for the car, things Tom typically would have done. He packed coolers, loaded luggage, and made many bathroom stops along the way with great patience. Tom Jr. was just too young for Disney World; he had just turned two, so we left him behind with Thelma. Although she was in deep grief, she was thrilled to be able to have him, and, in hindsight, the timing was perfect. Even though he was at a very demanding age, it gave her something to focus her love on, to hold and touch, at a very important time. It made her realize how important her grandchildren were in her life, and that they would become her primary focus after the enormous loss of her only son.

The trip was filled with realizations and healing at the

same time. Grief doesn't stay at home when you take a trip. It travels right beside you. It was the first small insight of how much I had relied on Tom. I felt like I was taking notes. Never go anywhere without another adult. The children were young, and just having help standing in line and getting tickets, or walking to the beach with towels, water, drinks, sunscreen, toys, etc., was a feat in itself, even with two other adults.

One morning after we had arrived in Destin, Bobby and Pam suggested that I go to the beach alone and take a book, just me, by myself, and stay as long as I wanted! It didn't take me long to respond! I felt like I was going on my own little trip. For a few hours, I only had to worry about me. I packed my straw bag with my latest self-help book, munchies, water, and my journal. I felt like I couldn't go anywhere without my journal; it was like my best friend! I stuffed in several towels and sunscreen, put on my hat and sunglasses, and off I went. I could hardly carry all the stuff. Bobby and Pam were probably wondering if I was leaving for days instead of hours! I felt guilty about being so excited. It was the first time I had felt that feeling of anticipation since Tom had died. I set off for the beach looking for a spot where there were not too many other people. This was my day to be truly alone, and I wanted to relish every moment of it.

When I reached the edge of the beach, I removed my sandals. As I walked, I felt the warm sand ooze between my toes. It startled me that I noticed the warmth, a new sensation; I was noticing feeling again. I looked around to find the perfect spot behind some large, white sand dunes. As I gazed out over the emerald blue water, it met the matching blue sky. It reminded me of infinity, no beginning and no end.

I sat down on the glistening, white sand and carefully placed all of my things around me on the towel, stretched out my legs, and felt my body go limp. The warm sand continued to enfold me and felt safe, like a blanket. I stared out at this endless infinity and took several deep breaths. As the tension started to leave my body, I realized it was the first time I had really completely relaxed since Tom had been diagnosed with cancer. It had been a roller coaster ride since then. I read and wrote many thoughts in my journal throughout that day. I didn't want to cry anymore; in fact, I wondered if I could have any tears left. I felt like a part of this landscape as I let the warm, soft, grainy sand seep through my fingers, and felt my body glisten with sweat from the hot sun. I noticed my deep breathing, and it made me realize the power and awareness of healing moments. I thought about listening to Tom's last breath and, now noticing my own breathing, that breath is really important, and how it connects us to all of life. Healing can't happen without this breathing, and it doesn't necessarily come in big chunks, but in small moments, such as this. I was melting into the beach like a grain of sand, understanding that I was a part of his greater creation, being alone with God and my thoughts, just me and him. I felt like I was in my own little Neverland, getting in touch with my own head and emotions. I would need many more moments and days in Neverland. This one day was worth the whole trip, and it was just the beginning of my little steps in the sand.

The year was a series of firsts. We had made it through summer. The trip to Florida had helped a lot. The next big hurdle was going to be the holidays. Just thinking about it made my stomach hurt. Thanksgiving was tolerable, but by far the hardest first was going to be Christmas. I was dreading the whole event. The thought of going to a Christmas party and pretending to be happy was more than I could handle. I also did not want people looking at me and feeling sorry for me. Tom had always lifted Melissa up to put the star on top of the tree. How was I going to handle that this year?

I knew my limitations. I knew that with the ages of my children, we would have to be at home for Christmas.

I was determined to give us all something to look forward to, so I planned a trip to Colorado with another family for the day after Christmas. I knew I was escaping, but I didn't care; it was the only way I could cope. Being away from familiar people and surroundings helped me put off some of the constant reminders of our enormous loss. I just wanted out of the pain. The trip turned out to be a positive experience. There were lots of people, outdoor activities, skiing, and hiking. I didn't stop missing Tom, but it was a welcome diversion before we returned home to familiar surroundings and challenges associated with this difficult path.

Several interesting events happened that fall after Tom's death, although, at the time, I did not know it, and actually connected me to the end of my journey. In early October, the local newspaper contacted me and wanted to do a story about grief during the holidays. The paper wanted to run this article from various perspectives on grief, and mine was to be the story on family grief. I willingly agreed, not knowing where my insight or answers would come from, but in hopes that the information could help others to know that someone else was making this journey and surviving. At the end of the article, I was quoted saying, "The next twenty years will be pretty much what I make it." When I made that statement, I was only six months into the grief process. This last year marked twenty years since Tom's death. Little did I know how true and powerful that statement was when I said it, and, how, twenty years later, it would underscore the significance of my journey and my understanding of it. Coincidence? I hardly think so.

The next trip I went on was to the Midwest, with the wife of my cousin. She had been through a similar experience only the year before. Her husband, my cousin, had been killed in a car wreck.

We went to her dad's house on a river in Michigan. I finally felt like I was with someone who understood. Losing a spouse at a young age makes you feel like you are out of step with the rest of the world. The trip was wonderful. We canoed down the river in the rain and rode bikes on beautiful trails. One night at dinner, she looked at my hand and asked me how long I was going to wear my wedding ring. I was startled. No one had ever broached this with me before. It had been about nine months since Tom had died. It was a gentle dose of reality that needed to happen. Knowing that she had "walked in my shoes" made it okay. I probably couldn't have heard that from someone else. The truth helped chip away at my denial.

Grief would overtake me at the oddest times, when I was least prepared. I was in the grocery store trying to decide what to buy for dinner. I would go down the aisles and start to put something in the basket and would say to myself, "No, I don't need that anymore, Tom isn't here to eat it." I'm sure I looked very confused and teary.

I signed up for a course that was designed to help people determine what to do with their lives. Little did I realize at the time, but I was still too overwhelmed to do that. It was too soon. Similar to being pregnant, you shouldn't make major decisions when you are first in grief. You are too emotional and driven. Your rational thinking is not at its best.

Toward the end of that first year, I enrolled in real estate school. After completing the course, I realized that with three young children, the weekends would not be the optimal time to be gone showing property. I could not be the parent I wanted to be and not be at home.
I desperately wanted to put my life back the way it had been before Tom died. I wanted out of the pain and the struggle. I was attempting to get clear on that vision, but it didn't seem to come easily.

Dating seemed to be a logical answer. Everyone kept saying, "You will meet the right person," and I completely believed that. Along with that belief, there seemed to be the thought that a woman could not raise a family alone. Of course, I believed that too.

That was when I met Joe. I was ecstatic! I couldn't believe I had met someone so soon; it had only been a little more than ten months since Tom's death. And I had just decided to stop wearing my wedding ring. How perfect! He had all the "right stuff." He was a doctor, well known in the community. I met him at the home of a friend at a party. It seemed like the perfect Cinderella story. He was divorced and had a family of his own. I thought I had been saved from the worst fate imaginable, being alone and raising my children. Fortunately, we dated long enough for me to realize that he was far from the right person for me and my children. As much as I wanted the relationship to work, it didn't. After having a really good relationship with Tom, I couldn't settle for something less. I couldn't believe someone had been put in my path that wasn't the right person. Why would God allow that to happen after all I had been through? It seemed totally unfair!

Dating brings all your loss issues roaring back to the surface, and mine had barely had time to be processed anyway. Dating made me feel vulnerable and fragile, but at the same time very alive. It was as if I needed to be reactivated as a person and a woman. Maybe that was the benefit to dating, although it made Tom's loss seem even bigger. I was trying to recreate my dream, and it wasn't working. I was being forced to see myself as the parent and provider for my children and to take responsibility for my own life. I could not fathom that I would ever have the tools to manage all of that alone. Over time, I came to realize a great truth: I was not managing this alone. God had carefully constructed my support system, both on earth, and on the "other side."

Tom and I had planned to remodel our home after the birth of young Tom. We only had three bedrooms, and with the large gaps in the ages of our children, we felt the children needed their own rooms. The plans were already in motion. Even though Tom had died, I saw no reason to stop the plans. I threw myself into remodeling. Tom had loved to build things. Remodeling was also a way to have a lot of activity around my house that reminded me of him. Grief takes lots of energy. The remodeling was somehow a way of keeping his spirit alive. At the time, remodeling and carrying forth his plans seemed like a completion of something that embodied part of him. On the other hand, remodeling also allowed me to focus on the permanency of my situation: another task I was attempting alone, another piece of acceptance.

The first year following Tom's death was finally over. It felt like the longest year of my life. Grief is messy. It is a grueling process that turns you inside out. All of the different experiences presented to me had allowed me to work through various emotions related to grief. The depth of my emotions sometimes scared me. I was by no means finished with grief, but I knew I had somehow made it through the first year. An interesting thing happened after that first year. I was starting to comprehend the enormity of what I had lost, and I knew I had no other choice but to go forward.

I was being challenged on every belief system that I had ever held. The questions kept rolling through my mind, "Where is God taking me?" and "Why did this happen to me?" It was as if God was taking me, whoever that was, apart, and putting me in a different package. I was ready to plug back into the blueprint I had designed for my life, but apparently God wasn't ready for me to go there, not just yet. I felt like Humpty Dumpty who had to be put back together again. All the visions and dreams about how life was supposed to be no longer fit. I had to look inside of the old box of beliefs I had lived with and decide what to keep on this next part of my journey. I was creating a new box, and it was very clear, many of my old beliefs simply wouldn't fit in the new box I was being handed. It was time to begin sorting.

Finding the Path

A VALLEY CAN BE SCARY. IT IS BIG AND WIDE, WITH LOTS OF TRAILS AND PATHS LEADING IN AND OUT. TRYING TO DETERMINE THE RIGHT TRAIL OR PATH THAT WILL LEAD UP AND OUT OF THE VALLEY, TOWARD THE TOP OF THE MOUNTAIN, IS THE CHALLENGE. IT IS CONFUSING, AND THE PATHS ALL LOOK SIMILAR FROM THE VIEW AT THE BOTTOM. YOU CAN'T TELL WHERE EACH PATH IS GOING. SOMETIMES YOU JUST HAVE TO START ON A PATH, OR CLEAR ONE FOR YOURSELF, IF YOU HAVE A GUT FEELING THAT IT WILL LEAD YOU OUT OF THE VALLEY AND UP THE MOUNTAIN.

My new path took the form of the graduate school of social work. It had been two years since Tom's death. After much soul-searching regarding my career, I applied to graduate school, and, much to my surprise, was accepted. I had good grades but had always been an average student, so the thought of graduate school felt intimidating. I had always been interested in counseling and had thought about pursuing that career after the children were in school, even when Tom and I were married. I envisioned a career path in private practice that would enable me to work and still have choices regarding my time and work schedule. This vision was being implemented sooner than I expected!

Graduate school was grueling, yet everything seemed to fall into place. My biggest dilemma was what to do with Tom, who was now in preschool. My days at school were long, and I could not be at his school in time to pick him up. It's the little pieces that have to be in place for a situation to work out. My friend Ginger rose to the challenge. She took Tom home from preschool every day so that I could go to my classes. Over the years Ginger became one of my closest friends and prayer partners, and remains so today. Except during Tom's illness, I had never had to rely upon or ask others for help, so this was a new shift for me. I was usually the one offering. I was beginning to understand what it meant to receive.

Graduate school was expanding my world. Walking on to the tree-lined campus seemed to fill my spirit with a sense of renewal. I had a study group that acted as a support system for one another. We were very diverse in our backgrounds, ideas, and ages, yet we were drawn together in this new arena. There was little time for anything other than graduate school and taking care of the children, yet I knew I needed other outlets.

In graduate school, I did a paper on the correlation between mental health, writing, and exercise. It became my mantra. We teach what we need to learn. When Tom had been so sick, it became paramount to me to maintain my health. Since my parents had passed away before Tom, and my siblings Mary and John did not live in the same city, I was always concerned about what would happen to my children if I got sick—another scary thought that lots of single parents face. Health was becoming a primary focus.

I thought about the beginning of Tom's illness, and the journaling I had done during that time. I realized that if I had the time and space to write and cry, I could function during other times. This outlet had kept me from losing my mind. When writing, I did not screen my emotions or feelings. It is like throwing up, it gets everything out. Expressing feelings keeps the chemistry in the body balanced and helps to sift through the emotions that control our mind. It is also best to write by hand so that the direction is from the subconscious.

As I journaled, I became clear and got answers to questions that were swimming around in my mind. It seemed as if this was another way of telling my story, which is an essential part of the grief process. Journaling helped me to understand my story and my emotions. I usually journaled at night, so that if I needed to cry, I could just allow myself to do that and not have to worry about what anybody thought.

As I told my story, I began to recognize the passage from one phase of grief to the next. Like a quilt, it enabled me to see the various threads in my life and where they were intersecting. It helped me to not just show up for the experience, but to feel the experience, so I realized I wasn't going crazy. It made what was happening to me real. At times, I would wonder if all this was really happening to me. My life had been so safe and normal before Tom's death. I wasn't sure what normal was anymore.

As I would write, the patterns emerged. They helped me gain a perspective on what was happening at a particular time in my life and explore the message or lesson attached to the experience. It helped me paint a picture of how my life really was, and what I had lost, which I now know is an essential part of the grief process that leads to acceptance. Looking at my losses wasn't easy. I had lost more than just Tom. I had lost the dream of my life and all that goes with that dream. That is a lot of loss. I had also not fully realized the impact of the loss of both my parents. This became magnified with the loss of Tom. I had lots of questions. Mainly, why had I been left so alone?

One day, my neighbor suggested I go with her to the park to start running. I informed her that I did not run. She said that I should come along and that I would be surprised by how far I could go. There was a whole world out there that I did not know existed! There were six or eight people that ran together everyday. At five thirty in the darkness of the morning, we would meet at a small parking lot. When I first began running, I could only run for about a mile. It wasn't long before I did three miles and then six. I loved running. I loved the sensation of stretching my body beyond its limits. I felt alive and was working out my anger on that path. The physical sensations of running, sweating, and feeling the humidity and dampness on your body at five thirty in the morning on a dirt path had a certain freedom, a cleansing sensation.

I was beginning to feel human again. Out here I was not a mother or a grieving widow. I was a runner, a free spirit, and I craved it. I also enjoyed the adult friendships. One man, Sam, an attorney, became a good friend and confidant. We ran as a pair every day, and at the same time had great conversations about everything from dating advice, to work, to world problems. We didn't solve the problems, but we tried. It further instilled in me the reality of my life as it was now, another little piece of acceptance, but in a positive way. I was not in a hurry to encounter another relationship either, and it was a way to have some great friendships. There is something very refreshing and honest about running with people at five thirty in the morning—there are no masks!

Grief lodges itself in our cellular body. Just as the endorphins are released when we exercise, when we grieve, our mind and body release chemicals that tell all of the cells that we are grieving. Exercise became another tool to help me to keep my body chemistry in balance while the strong emotions of anger, sadness, anxiety, and depression were raging.

The other outlet that became important to me was going to lunch. My children were so far apart in age and involved in so many activities that socializing in the evenings was difficult. It takes time to maintain friendships. We all have to eat, so the main time I could connect with my friends was at lunch.

This was my other world. These "lunch ladies" were the women who had supported me during Tom's illness, the ones who had helped me get the children to T-ball practice, and the ones who prayed with me. Maintaining these friendships also helped me to bridge my connection and identity with the two worlds that I was merging together. My friendships were changing as well. It was not easy for my friends to grasp the enormity of what had happened to me and how much my life had changed. I would find myself being resentful at times, knowing they still had what I had lost. I am sure the reality of my situation was scary and uncomfortable for them; it was for me, too. We were all struggling to find some meaning out of this experience. I was beginning to understand that grief touches every level of our being, physically, emotionally, and spiritually. Bruce Lipton, Ph.D., author of *The Biology of Belief*, explains how thoughts and feelings affect the cellular level, and how our DNA changes, depending on what you think and feel.

My priorities were really changing. Journaling, exercise, and going to lunch became the greater part of my stability, my lifeline. I had never looked at my own needs. I had been so focused on surviving and the needs of the children after the death, I realized that exercising and adult companionship were meeting some of my most basic needs. I was beginning to understand that I was on a path that was pulling me along to become an entirely different person from the young woman who had married, had a successful husband, and had stayed home with her children.

The enormity of my new path felt daunting and scary. I would lie in my bed in the morning and say, "Okay God, You put me here. Now how am I going to handle this?" Or, "Now it's gone too far. What am I going to do?" If I thought God didn't hear me, I would talk to Tom. Almost every day! After all, he said he would never leave me. I was taking him at his word. Without other family support, God and Tom became my main confidants. Each new situation was helping me accept the reality that this was the life I had been handed, and nothing I could do was going to change that reality. But I also knew I couldn't do this alone. I was becoming aware that my confidants on the other side were constantly vigilant.

It's easy to focus on the negative. In fact, it is almost as if we are trained to look at the gaps in our lives. As important as it was to look at what I had lost, it now became paramount to look at what I had left. I knew that I would never make it if I only looked at the losses. So I began to look at what was left in my life. I had my house, my children, my health, and some money. That is a lot in the scheme of things. My children still went to the same school. To help me begin to focus on the positive, I started to make a list and write down the good things I had in my life. There was a whole new world being presented to me, and I had to look at what I had left as if it were a ball of clay that I needed to mold into something new.

I could feel myself resisting this new life. I spent a lot of time thinking about how to plug back into my old life, but no amount of scheming seemed to work. This new life was not the one I had designed. I was not sure if I wanted to go forward, although going backward did not seem like an option either. I felt like Alice in Wonderland. The door to the unknown was opening, but I didn't know if I was brave enough to enter. I didn't know what was on the other side. But somewhere inside of me, I knew that God did know where I was going. So, I felt that I had no other choice. I kept opening the door and following the path that appeared in front of me.

During the next few years, my life changed dramatically. I realized the word *growing* did not mean obtaining more—it actually meant letting go, as my lifestyle changed. It was the simple things I really missed. I missed the intimacy of my relationship with Tom—the physical touch, having him just holding, hugging, and touching me. When I would come home in the afternoons and see the neighbors sitting on their driveways, I was reminded that I did not have as much time for all of the things that had been a part of my former life, such as chatting with the neighbors, or just being at home cooking, or having the leisure of watching a talk show, or going to the farmers market. As I prepared dinner for three hungry children after running in the door at five thirty, my new life became a stark reality. Just who designed this plan anyway! It certainly wasn't me. What was the reason for this difficult journey? I felt compelled to find some answers to these difficult questions, to make sense of all this. Carl Jung says that there are two parts to our lives: the exterior journey, which is defined by possessions and things of the world; and the interior journey to the center of our being. I was definitely embarking on the latter. This was not a journey for the faint of heart. The completion of graduate school felt like a huge milestone. It was hard to believe that almost five years had passed since Tom's death. I interviewed and began my first job after graduate school. The position was at a social service agency as a beginning therapist. I had never really worked since I had children, and I had no realistic expectation of what balancing a career, children, and a home would require. I had never aspired to have a career and be a super mom. The salaries at the social service agency were less than ideal, but the experience was necessary to move forward in the profession. It was similar to working in the emergency room of a charity hospital. The needs are tremendous and overwhelming. I felt unprepared and enormously challenged. The question kept burning in my mind, "How am I ever going to do this and raise a family?" All of the sudden, there was not enough money or time.

All of my life I had heard people say, "If he brings us to it, he will bring us through it." I was counting on that. I was really trusting that he would keep his end of the bargain. Even though I was apprehensive about where this path was taking me, people seemed to keep appearing that were able to help me with the next steps. That is when I met my wonderful supervisor at the agency, Madeline. She was a nun who had been a former policewoman in Chicago. She was mother earth and leader to a whole group of inexperienced therapists who had just come to the agency out of graduate school. Our work at the agency was intense, and our group bonded quickly and became very close. Similar to my fellow students in graduate school, we acted as an incredible support system for each other. Our situations were similar in that we were individuals who had returned to school for one reason or another, had families, and were entering the workforce in a new field. We were all juggling to make our lives work.

Acting as a responsible parent and still doing a good job at the agency seemed to be the immediate pressure and challenge. I thought about all the men I had known who acted as the primary support for their families. I was gaining a new respect and understanding of how they must feel. Big expectations and pressure! We had to be there several nights a week, and the work load was huge. I presented my dilemma to my supervisor, Madeline. I talked to her about my carpools, sports events, and other child-related responsibilities, but also about my commitment to do an excellent job. She helped me design a schedule that would work for both of us. Some nights I went back to the agency and worked after my afternoon carpool duties. I definitely put in my time but felt that my children were getting their needs met as well. It wasn't easy, but it worked! Little did I realize it at the time, but I was creating choices. Each choice always seemed to lead me in a new direction. Not big choices, but small, everyday choices that have a great affect upon our lives, and the outcome and rhythm of how we live. On the days that I felt stretched and overwhelmed by the new path that lay before me, I had to pull back and repeat the words, "small choices, small steps," like my small steps in the Florida sand. Learning to focus on the small choices made the bigger picture more palatable and less daunting for me. It was scary, but I kept walking on the path.

I was trying to stay involved in the children's activities. I really looked forward to Saturday mornings. The sports leagues the children played in were usually on Saturday, so I knew I could always be there for those games. Like many parents, it is a great challenge to get to the games during the week. There was so much I used to take for granted. Once again, the simple stuff, like being a room mother, or helping to the read a story in Tom's kindergarten class, required precise scheduling now. That never used to be the case.

One day, Tom's kindergarten teacher called me. It was near Thanksgiving, and she explained that the next week at school Tom had a project that involved drawing his family. She was concerned that this would be confusing for him, and possibly upsetting. Thank God for this wise teacher! Her compassion and insight were absolutely on target. I would have never thought about this on my own. We developed a plan that would include me coming to school and helping with his drawing of our family and helping him use language in a way that he could explain it. He had a very limited concept of what a dad was at this point. He had not yet entered into the activities that made him understand the enormity of what had happened and what he had lost. Since Tom had only been a little more than a year old when his father died, the understanding of the role a father plays in a family was unknown to him. He did not really understand the permanency of death, or the part it played in our family. He was not grieving at this stage like a child who would have known his father. I realized that he would fully experience grief when he understood the loss at later developmental stages.

I took on the task of helping him to draw his family, and to understand how to find words to explain to the other children why his family picture looked different from their pictures. Not many five-year-old children have a missing parent. In the simplistic language of children, we helped him explain that his father was in heaven, which was exactly where he drew him, and that the rest of his family lived together in our house. No big words needed here, just keep it simple. Once again, because of the wonderful people put in my path—Madeline, my insightful supervisor, providing great support and flexibility, and a wise and caring kindergarten teacher—we gently guided Tom through what could have been a very difficult experience. Once again, small pieces had to fall into place to make my two worlds work, and they did.

I had a lot of responsibility at work, and needless to say, I wanted to prove that I could handle it. The tasks were all new to me and so was the arena. It was my job to oversee a group program that involved a contract with the state. It was enormous, and people from all over the city participated one night a week. Some of these participants were less than trustworthy, but I had a big trust level. One evening, as the people were beginning to go to their groups, I noticed something sticking out of the back of a man's coat. Several people thought it was a gun. In my innocence, I thought that if it was a gun, he would understand that he would have to turn it over to me. After all, I was in charge! I approached this man and politely asked him to come with me into an office. I closed the door after he entered the room, and informed him that he had to give me the gun. No arguments. Just hand it over. He slowly started to pull the object out of the back of his coat. I thought my life was going to be over. But, as he reached behind his back he was gently explaining that it was an umbrella. My stomach dropped. I had a lot to learn! My days of being naïve were coming to an end. I stayed at the agency for three years, and during that time became supervisor of the child abuse program. Similar to graduate school, opportunities began to flow. I was beginning to notice that doors seemed to open with ease, and this natural flow would just happen when everything worked.

I was starting to understand that this journey was not just about Tom's death, it was really about my life. The years at the agency were a time to prepare me for and to adjust to this new life that I was creating. My image of myself was changing. I had transitioned into a new role as a provider, but with that understanding, came the huge realization that being a mom who was available and present was possible as well. All the pieces were being put into place so that I could achieve balance and be supported. God didn't miss a beat, a day or a detail, and if I thought he did, I had a real heart-to-heart talk with him! Both parts, provider and mother, had to be supported for me to feel good about myself.

It made me start to question myself, "What part of my old beliefs and identities still fit in this new person? What beliefs do I need to let go of that no longer fit and work to support where I am in my life now?" Like trying on new clothes, I had to get rid of some of the old ones to make room for the new. My mother had been the typical fifties mom and stayed home with her children. My belief was that it couldn't work any other way. Boy, was I being proven wrong, and that was only the beginning!

My children were "changing their clothes" as well. We were all moving on in different ways. As each child reached a new developmental place, we encountered new issues related to grief. This was my biggest surprise.

It is never really just "over." Grief turns us inside out, and when one child would finish a situation, another would begin. It was as if these situations were presented to help us grieve. Just when you think you are over certain hurdles, it grabs you again. I had many times that I called "parent moments" that pulled up enormous, big tears. These are the kind of tears you try to hold back and just can't; they just come rolling out of your eyes. These are special moments in a child's life that only a parent can appreciate or understand.

Kelly, my oldest, called me at work one afternoon with the news that she was trying out for school cheerleader. I was in my first year of work at the agency, and she had just transferred to a large public high school near our home. I said, "Kelly, don't get your hopes up. You only know a handful of people in your new school." I couldn't bear the thought of her being hurt and disappointed again after what she had been through with her dad only a few years before. No parent wants to see their child hurting. I knew she had been practicing, but I didn't know she had intended to participate in the tryouts so soon. The tryouts were that afternoon. I guess she waited to tell me so I wouldn't put a damper on her efforts. Sometimes I would try to protect too much. After all, isn't a parent supposed to know best? Fortunately she followed her own intuition.

I walked into the auditorium late in the afternoon for the tryouts and stood in the back. We were new to the high school, and I knew no one else there. The building was packed with students, teachers, and parents. The energy in the auditorium was electric, like something out of a movie. Several students who had been trying out to be cheerleader had just left the stage. People were yelling and cheering. The next name called was Kelly's. I had gotten there just in time. I felt a huge knot in the pit of my stomach. I just hoped she wouldn't fall down. I had never seen her do her routine. I leaned against the back wall of the steamy auditorium and held my stomach, thinking about my worst fears. What if she fell down, what if no one clapped, what if, what if, what if?

All of a sudden, I saw this person I had never really seen before. She was doing flips, yelling, and totally captivating and engaging her audience. Within the next five minutes, the whole auditorium was on its feet, yelling and moving with her. I couldn't believe what I was witnessing—she was awesome! Wow! And, she won! I kept thinking, "I can't believe that is my daughter!" The next thought caught me off guard, as my eyes filled with big tears, and I looked around, and I realized I had no one to share that very special moment with, that big parent moment.

Not all parent moments are happy occasions. One evening, when Tom Jr. was in third grade, I was waiting in the car for him after basketball practice. He came rushing out to the car crying. He started yelling and burst into tears. He said, "I'm not good enough to play! If only I had a dad to practice with, I would be better. I am never going to play again!"

Even though my heart was breaking, I knew I could not let him dissolve in self-pity. One of my biggest concerns and fears was raising a son without a father. The stories I had heard about this were not very positive. To help Tom keep the situation in perspective, I asked him how many players in the NBA, or any other sport for that matter, had a dad that came home and shot hoops with them every evening? I also told him I knew it was really tough not having a dad to be there for him when he needed support.

There were many times like this that his grief came rushing to the surface and would completely overwhelm him. I was learning that children grieve in spurts and according to their own developmental timetable. At each stage, they have a different concept of what they have lost. Watching my children navigate their various developmental stages once again raised my awareness of the powerful impact that grief has on our lives and the formation of our identity. Capturing the concept of self-identity can be challenging for a child when a primary identity figure is no longer a part of their life. We had many long discussions and told stories about their dad, to help the children understand who that person really was, and to capture the memory in many different ways. Being realistic was important—as was not putting him on a pedestal they couldn't reach.

The one priority that I knew had to stay in place was an emphasis on family. Tom and I had been very focused on family, always planning activities that included the children. I knew that if my children were okay, I would be okay. I have always heard, "We are only as happy as our unhappiest child"—that was me. I was aware of how much more difficult this would be, both as a single parent, and with not having my own extended family close by. Even though we were few in numbers, I wanted to make it clear to them how important it was to support each other as a family. The challenge was to find ways we could all agree upon to do that. No longer having a lake house and some of the other amenities, we had to be creative about how we could spend time together as a family.

Our weeks were all so busy that it was difficult to find one time that we would be together for sharing a meal.

That was the beginning of Sunday Night Dinner. The children always invited friends, and through the years, it became fun, gathering to see who showed up on Sunday night. It was always a surprise!

Rituals are important, and Sunday Night Dinner was a great way to experience a new ritual for our family. Everyone had a part in the dinner, whether setting the table, cooking, or bringing a new dessert. If you came for dinner, you had to help, no exceptions! As we gathered around the table, we always started with a prayer, usually spontaneous. That honor was offered to whatever extra person happened to show up as a guest. The food was passed, along with the jokes, as everyone tried to one up each other with a great weekend story—but always trying to cover up incidents and information, so that I would not figure out details I wasn't supposed to know. The stories usually ended in lots of laughter, which gave me wonderful insights into my children's lives. It was at this table that we learned about manners and relationships and trust. It was a great way for all of us to start the week.

I finally felt like my family was beginning to stabilize again. We were coming out of the valley. Every event did not seem like a crisis or a roller-coaster ride. It wasn't like it was before, but it was okay. That was when I decided that I was finally ready to look for Mr. Right.

Climbing the Mountain

The Land of the Unknown

I KNEW I WAS READY TO TAKE THE PLUNGE AGAIN INTO THE WORLD OF DATING. I FELT LIKE MY ARMOR WAS STRONG ENOUGH TO HANDLE IT NOW. I WENT OUT WITH SEVERAL MEN WHO WERE NOT MR. RIGHT, AND THEN I MET RUSTY.

My doorbell rang. He was supposed to pick me up at noon to go to Galveston for the afternoon. I opened the door, and he greeted me in his shorts and flip flops. He was tall and had a big smile. As we drove to the beach, the conversation never lagged. We had a lot in common. His wife had recently died. He had two daughters who were close in age to mine. As we walked on the beach he held my hand. It had been a long time since someone held my hand. It felt safe and caring; I had missed that a lot. The day unfolded in a timeless, easy way. We went to dinner, and I realized that I did not even know his last name!

Rusty was from a small town in Texas west of Houston. One of my closest friends had fixed me up with him. He was similar to Tom in some ways. He was financially stable, loved golf, and was a simple, down-to-earth person. My kids enjoyed him a lot. He took Tom Jr. on hunting and fishing trips. It seemed like a great fit. And, I did want to get married again. We dated for about a year. Over that year, we discovered some differences that seemed to be bigger than we were. We danced around the subject of marriage, but it just didn't seem to be the right move for us. Something in my gut—and his—said that this was not the thing to do. We mutually agreed, and broke off the relationship. I wondered if we were soul mates. Soul mates don't always stay together. We learned what we needed to learn from each other. I had lots of salty tears. I was disappointed, but not devastated. I guess I had healed enough over the past several years not to be devastated. That was a positive sign. It just wasn't meant to be, at least not at that time. As much as I still wanted my Cinderella story to manifest itself, the person had to be right. And you know when it's not. I was back on an uncharted path.

Dating was not easy! I dated, but the continual question, "Is he the right one?" was always ringing in my ears. I would think someone would have just the right qualities, and then something just wouldn't fit. Questions about how to involve or not involve the children always surfaced. It just wasn't an easy call. How could God take Tom and leave me to raise these kids alone? According to my plan, that wasn't the way it was supposed to be. Could it be that God was trying to tell me something different? Was I supposed to develop a higher level of trust with him? Was it possible that I was supposed to raise these children alone? I spent many hours asking God and my other confidant, Tom, for these answers. There are some questions that have no obvious answers, and you have to wait for the answer to unfold. That requires patience, which is a quality that I struggle with a lot.

I began to understand that the things I struggled with were the things that led me inward to search for answers. I was being led into situations and circumstances that seemed beyond my understanding. This difficult place is often referred to as the "dark night of the soul." We will all journey there at some point, and the only way out is to go through. I found that if I ignored a difficult situation or ran away from it, the same circumstance would be presented to me again, but the challenge would become even greater. I was learning to try and get it right the first time—the replays were tough.

When Alice looked into the looking glass, what did she see? I was looking into my looking glass, and I was not seeing the same person who had been there a few years before. I was not sure exactly who this person would be at the end of this process, but it hardly resembled the person I had been. During my marriage to Tom, I had identified myself by his career, our church, and our possessions. We had a lake house, a bay house, and were in the process of acquiring much more. Tom was very good at what he did, and was on the fast track in his career. I was right beside him. Now the doors of my golden cage had been thrown open. Dating forces you to look at yourself in a whole new way, and it felt very vulnerable.

Many of the exterior sources by which I had identified myself and my world were gone. I was now being forced to turn inward and search deeper for qualities that identified me. Certainly, I had been forced into new roles. Many of the skills I had used in other areas of my life, such as volunteer work, now translated into marketable job skills.

I was learning, through journaling and prayer, to follow my gut and let go of some of the control or, better yet, the illusion of control. Watching Tom die made me realize we have control over nothing. Control feels like security, which is predictable, and nothing in my life felt very predictable anymore. I was beginning to understand that someone else was truly in charge. I wasn't just giving lip service to that belief, I was calling on God daily for my guidance. But to access and call on God, I had to look inward, not outward. Looking inward meant finding that center inside of myself, and understanding that my center was greater than just my physical self. My center is connected to the universe, which is connected to my Higher Power. I could no longer live in my golden cage.

Grief was pushing my spirituality to a new level. My spirituality was expanding far beyond the more conservative religious beliefs that I had embraced in my earlier years. In creating this new blueprint for my life, I was beginning to understand that having everything work out perfectly in all areas of my life is not necessarily the path that is going to lead me to the spiritual depth necessary to enable me to understand my soul or my purpose. I was being pushed into the land of the unknown. It seemed to me that Tom's death did not leave me with a lot of good choices, or choices I liked, or, more importantly, choices that felt familiar to me. But, I did have choices. I hear a lot of people say, "I just did not have a choice." We may not like the choice, but we always have one. I knew that I was learning life lessons that were necessary for my soul to evolve. Since I did not have my parents or Tom to turn to, I grappled for my answers in prayer. It became my avenue for my truth. As much as I resisted examining the answer to that continuous question, "Why did this happen to me?" that question was beginning to make more sense. Would I have ever grappled for answers in prayer if I never left the land of the known?

Growing up as a Catholic with structured prayer had laid the foundation for what was to come in my spiritual life. I had been a part of a Bible study group when Tom got sick, and had also been in a group called Thersians. This was a Catholic women's group based on the values of St. Theresa. My Thersians group and my Bible study group had prayer partners whom you could call on for special requests. It was no mistake that I was in both groups when Tom got sick, and there is no doubt that their prayers and God's grace helped carry my family through that difficult period.

I was realizing that, in addition to running and lunch, I had to prioritize times to pray. My time was so limited that if I did not schedule something in my day, it simply did not happen. Several of my current prayer partners were people I had not known before Tom's death. Once again, the right people seemed to show up according to the need that I had at that time. Karen was one of these people. She would meet me at my home during the day on a weekly basis. As our prayers were answered,

I would share these insights with my children. At the time, I had no idea of the profound impact that this prayer life had on my children. They were able to witness the amazing outcomes of those prayers. It didn't mean things always worked out, but I knew that if I prayed, the right choice for that moment would be presented to me. There was no shortage of requests!

I was beginning to understand that our Father has no covenant to answer prayers of the ego, or to make fictions result in happiness, or to honor anything that would separate us from him. When I hear someone talking about what they are lacking in life, whether it is health, money, or happiness—or whatever it is that seems to be a problem—it is probably the very thing that is going to push them along on their path and into a closer relationship with God. He is begging us to turn it over to him. He wants us close, really close. That is when we have to enter the land of the unknown.

I really saw the implications of my prayer life when I had a challenge with my health. My health has probably been one of my greatest blessings. I was in shock when I went to the doctor with what I thought was a bladder infection, and it turned out to be a large cyst on my ovary. He recommended immediate surgery. I did not want the surgery, which translated into time off from work, money, and fear. I went to two other doctors, and both recommended the same thing, except that one said I could watch it for a few weeks. He said that if the cyst would decrease, I could treat it differently. I was scared! A health issue for a surviving, single parent is huge!

A friend of mine suggested I go see a woman named Emily, who did healing work. At the time, I did not understand healing work, and was very apprehensive, but decided to try it anyway. If there was an outside chance that I could avoid surgery, I was willing to try it. Over the next few weeks, Emily worked with me and opened my energy systems. She helped me understand that everything she did was only in addition to anything traditional medicine was doing, which at that moment was just waiting.

Each time I would go to Emily, she worked on my chakra centers. The chakra centers are the seven, main energy centers in the body. It made perfect sense that after all of the trauma I had been through, my energy centers would be blocked. The premise is that any emotions and feelings we do not process or express are stored in our bodies. Each chakra is connected to a certain part of the body. If our energy or chakra centers are blocked in our bodies, it can manifest itself as illness, depression, or general dysfunction in our life. Lying on a table as she worked, I would go into a semimeditative state during the session. Emily would talk with me about where she felt blockage and try to help me discover the reason for that particular blockage. This was my introduction to meditation and healing work. I would continue my own meditation and energy work during the week after I would meet with her. I felt better and better. I knew something had happened.

I went back to the doctor six weeks later, and he did a sonogram on my ovary to determine if I needed the surgery. He appeared to be shocked and said, "Your cyst is completely gone. What did you do?" I told him a little about the energy work Emily had used on me. He just shook his head in disbelief. I was ecstatic!

This was another huge turning point for me. I had trusted my guidance and intuition that led me to Emily, and to my connection with God. Like other aspects of our spirituality, information has to be presented when we are ready to receive it. The journey of grief turns our old paradigms and belief systems upside down. I had to alter the way I looked at the world and the myths of my earlier years. The priorities of what was important in my life had changed dramatically, along with my identity.

Our neighborhood was an important part of our world

and identity. One of our neighbors, Rosie, was a beautiful Italian lady with silver gray hair. She lived next door. Nothing escaped her watchful eye. She was like a grandmother to all my children, but especially to Tom. From the day he came home from the hospital, she would sit and rock him until he fell asleep. She owned rental property and would often take Tom with her as she went to collect her rent. She fascinated him. He had never known a lady who could stand up to almost any man she met, kept a pistol under her front car seat, and let him take candy out of the jar in her kitchen any afternoon he happened to wander over to her house. When I couldn't find Tom, I knew where he was—at Rosie's, eating candy and watching TV. For a six-year-old boy, it doesn't get any better than that. They had a special relationship. He thought she was the coolest woman he had ever met. She was one of many neighbors who were like best friends.

I was realizing that the more I said yes to God, the more we were surrounded with people on our journey to help carry us. I wasn't sure where God was taking me, but I was a little more willing to trust. After all, I had no one else to rely on but him. I felt like I was holding on to new threads in the quilt, and it was creating a new design. I still had a lot to learn.

For a period of time it became more and more evident

that many of the experiences on my path were leading me into and through this dark night. I knew it was a dark night when I wanted to give up completely, when I saw no light, no choices. It felt as if praying was not helping, and no one was hearing me. I wondered if God, Tom, and all my spiritual supports had deserted me. The path was still guiding me into rocky territory. I was placing one foot in front of the other and trying to stay on the path. There were no other options than to go forward; there was no reverse.

Over the next few years, I was forced to make some difficult choices. I was definitely struggling through one of my dark nights. Tom had always taken care of our finances when we were married. I didn't really have to worry about how the bills were getting paid, or generate the income to do so. We had been a very young couple when Tom had died, so we had not had the opportunity to save a lot, and even though we had some life insurance, I was left with the task of trying to manage a family on one income. I knew that going back to school had been a good choice, but because of that, combined with working at a social service agency for three years and supporting three children, my resources had dwindled. It had been seven years since Tom had died, and I knew that I would have to sell my home that we had lived in for fourteen years.

I was devastated and felt like a failure. I spent hours retracing and questioning all my decisions, trying to determine what I could have done differently. The house also represented my last attachment to my former life with Tom. I knew somehow I had to find the strength to go on, or give up completely. I mentally made the shift and decided to go on, even though it felt hopeless. Things were not working out the way I had planned.

I thought we had healed a lot over the past few years, but the idea of moving seemed to bring all of our loss issues rushing to the surface again. My house was on the market for a long time. I had no idea where we would go, or if I could find another home in the area I wanted that we could afford. I looked at tons of properties, and none seemed to be just right. Lots of questions and big decisions lay ahead of me. It was a stressful time, dealing with the emotional attachment and identity I felt with both my neighborhood and my house. Once again, I questioned why I felt like I was being forced to leave a place where we had been so happy. My children were angry about moving as well. It felt like we were letting go of another piece of our identity and security, and we were.

I had a lot of support, but no one could change the inevitable. We had to move. It was a relief when the house finally sold. After months of looking, I noticed a for sale sign in a neighborhood close to the children's school. Finding a house in an area near the children's school was paramount to me. It was by far the most unattractive house that I had looked at; it even had an orange front door! But something kept drawing me to it, and, besides the location, it had one feature I couldn't ignore. As I walked into the den, the house had a space in the wall, like a bookcase, which was exactly the right size for a boat in a glass case that was an heirloom from Tom's family. One of my biggest dilemmas was where I was going to put this boat when we moved. It was no small object! In my confusion, the opening seemed like a beacon in the night to pull me toward this house. The captain seemed to still be at the helm guiding this ship through this dark night.

The other big factor was the location—it was perfect. The house was near the school Tom still attended. Kelly had just left for college, Melissa would be entering high school, and Tom still attended a parochial school, that he had attended since kindergarten. The house was near carpools and friends that were a key part of their support system and mine.

It didn't take long for me to make a decision. My realtor was out of town, but my cousin, who was also a realtor, offered to help me complete the deal. The day I submitted a contract on the house, she informed me someone else had submitted another contract offer the same day. The other contract offer was for more money than mine. I was totally discouraged. I thought, "What are my chances? No one turns down more money." I was sure I did not have a chance. Even though I wasn't in love with the house, I knew it had potential, and the basic right stuff! It was the perfect sleeper in this desirable neighborhood.

A few weeks prior to my offer, my original realtor had suggested I submit a letter to go with the contract explaining why I wanted the house, and a little about my situation. I thought that the idea was pretty hopeless, but I really wanted this house, so I did what she suggested. I wrote an honest letter explaining why this particular house was important to me, including the location to the children's school, my life as a single parent, and the opening for the boat. Little did I know the impact my letter would make on the seller. I didn't have to wait long for an answer. The next day the agent called and said that the owner of the house accepted my contract over the other one.

I found out later that it was nothing short of a miracle that I got this house. Little did I know, but the owner of the house was a very spiritual man, and reading my letter touched his heart. I was amazed at the way my answer had been provided. I was grateful that I was coming out of this dark night. I knew, once again, we had been held in the palm of God's hand. Amazing things happen when he is in charge!

At this point, I thought that I had learned every lesson God could possibly want me to learn. I had entered the land of the unknown, not willingly, but at least I didn't turn back. My husband had died, I had gone back to school and to work, and I'd sold my house. My identity had changed, and I had opened myself to the new values and priorities that had been presented to me. Even though I was scared of the future, I was learning to let go of the past, which had brought my spirituality to a new depth. I had learned that Tom's pledge that he would never leave me held much more truth than I ever imagined. Without completely understanding how, I had formed a new relationship with him. We communicated frequently. What else could I possibly be presented with in this life path?

It didn't seem as if my friends had to learn all of this difficult stuff; why me? Maybe my Higher Power just felt that I had a lot of stuff that needed fixing or that he was refining me. God reminds me of the alchemist, refining us to find the gold inside ourselves. I analyzed every situation and determined that he surely must be finished with his product. I was so relieved, I truly felt there couldn't be anything else, and I was finished. It was then I learned that God doesn't follow our perception of being finished.

Signs on the Path

I COULDN'T BELIEVE EIGHT YEARS HAD PASSED SINCE TOM'S DEATH. THE NEW HOUSE WAS A BLESSING, BUT LEAVING THE OLD NEIGHBORHOOD AND FRIENDS HAD BEEN HARD, A BIG TRANSITION FOR ALL OF US. I FELT AS IF I HAD UNDERGONE SOME TYPE OF RITE OF PASSAGE. I HAD SAID SO MANY GOODBYES. I WAS TRULY COMMITTED TO EVERY ASPECT OF MY NEW LIFE, SPIRITUALLY, MENTALLY, AND PHYSICALLY.

The new house was not as big as the old one. The children had to share bathrooms again, and other space. No one had as much privacy. Even though Kelly had left for college, Melissa and Tom had to share space for the first time. For Melissa, now a freshman in high school, this was the ultimate frustration! Her losses were being brought up all over again. The stark reality remained that if she had not lost her father, none of this would have happened. Her anger and tears were understandable. Even though it had been eight years, she was grieving again through a new lens, that of a fourteen-year-old.

My life and choices were now being driven and balanced by more of an internal, rather than, external force. During the same time period that I had to move and sell my house, I decided to pursue private practice, which had always been my desire. I had been at the agency for three years and was ready to use what I had been learning in a different way. I also knew I had to increase my income, and private practice could definitely provide that opportunity. By now, I was starting to trust my intuition and my heart.

Something inside kept nagging at me to call a professional in my field named Suzanne. I had heard her name over and over. I did not know her personally, but her reputation was excellent. It wouldn't hurt to just talk with her about her successful practice. Perhaps she could give me some advice about how to break into the field, or maybe she would have a small bit of available contract work, just to help me get my feet wet. I knew she had done what I dreamed of doing, starting a private practice. I gathered up my courage and called, and she agreed to at least talk with me.

I walked into her beautiful office. It overlooked a lake

with wildlife and ducks swimming. It was a therapist's dream. I was not prepared for what happened next. We connected well and talked for more than an hour. We realized that we shared a lot in common. She had also worked at the social service agency where I was employed and had stayed for three years. She had also been raising a family alone after a divorce. It turned out that the two people who had worked with Suzanne for several years in her private practice were leaving her group. They had informed her of this decision the week before I came to meet with her. She asked me how soon I could transition out of the agency. I couldn't believe my ears! It reinforced my belief that there are no coincidences. I followed my heart, and God had the bigger plan, which he could now unfold. I was the replacement!

I was starting to pay more attention to signs. I love signs. Everyone who knows me knows that I watch and usually get certain signs about things I am praying about. Some signs point us in another direction or simply let us know that we are on the right path. Signs should not control us, but simply give us hope, or gently push us in a certain direction and give us affirmation that we are on the right path.

I started to notice that every day, a beautiful cardinal came to the same hanging basket outside my patio door.

I couldn't figure out why it kept coming; then I saw it. The cardinal had made a nest in the basket. Somehow my intuition kept telling me it was all connected to something bigger that was happening.

Thelma, my mother-in-law, to whom I was still very close, was in a nursing home. When Thelma had lived at home, she had pictures of cardinals and statues of cardinals—she loved them. They were her favorite bird, and whenever I saw a cardinal, I thought of Thelma. I had been sensing that Thelma wasn't going to be alive much longer. She had been in a nursing home with Alzheimer's disease for the past few years. Somehow I knew this cardinal making its nest had something to do with her. I also knew it had a message for me. I had to watch closely and quietly to get the message.

The cardinal brought a second bird, her mate, and she sat quietly every day on the two precious little eggs. Mandy, our golden retriever that had been a gift to our family, watched the cardinal too, but she never interfered with what was going on. It never seemed to frighten the cardinal that mandy was practically stationed under her nest. Mandy would sit patiently and watch and wait with the cardinals. I was getting anxious about what would happen when the eggs actually hatched. What if a bird fell out? What if I wasn't home?

Would mandy kill the little cardinals? I wasn't sure what the message or the outcome would be. The only thing I was sure of was that this process had a very important message for me, being driven from something I did not totally understand. I also knew that I had no control over the outcome. My job was to watch, listen, and learn from this miracle of nature unfolding on my patio.

Finally the eggs hatched! I think I was as excited as the mother bird. In fact, at this point, my whole family was watching this little miracle every day! We watched as the devoted parents brought food to the little nest several times a day. Mandy grew nervous and paced when the young birds would cry waiting on their mother. My thoughts kept gravitating back to Thelma. What was she trying to tell me?

After several days, the little birds were sticking their necks out and trying to lift their bodies and legs. Then, one morning, one little bird fell out of the nest. He flapped, but he didn't go anywhere. The mother and the father would fly back and forth to the patio and fly up and down, trying to show him what to do. Mandy and I watched from the breakfast room window as a lesson in Life 101 started to unfold. I found myself saying, "It's time for you to go, just watch your parents." Animals have a wonderful way of trusting that their offspring have been given all the resources to do what they need to do, and at the right time. Was that the lesson for me?

By the afternoon he was flying. I was so proud of him, as I'm sure his parents were too! I kept mandy inside, for her natural instincts could only be tested so far. Now what was going to happen to the other sibling, the one that was left behind? The parents kept returning to the nest to bring food. I kept asking myself, "Will this one make it?" I had thought the same thing about myself many times, wondering if I would make it with the path I had been handed. How many times had I thought about giving up? About four days later, the last little bird literally fell out of the nest. The mother bird was right there, flying around and trying to help the second little bird figure out what to do. The father would come when the mother would leave, walking around, flying, chirping, trying everything he knew to teach the little bird. But this little bird didn't get it as easily. For days, the little bird would hide under tables on the patio, get scared and distracted, and sit and chirp and cry. It seemed like he was paralyzed by fear. The other baby bird had flown so easily, why was it so hard for this one?

Again, I thought about myself. So many times my path had seemed more difficult than others, or at least I perceived it that way. How many times had I been paralyzed by fear, just like this little bird? I realized that during those times of fear, I had been protected, just like I was protecting the little bird from mandy. Finally, the little bird started to flap his wings. He took a small hop, then a bigger hop; he was trying! The whole family became his cheering squad, as we stood at the window saying, "You can do it! Just let go and fly!" It took several days, but he finally took a big hop, lifted those little wings and took off.

The next week Thelma died. There were many lessons unfolding during this month with the cardinals. I was sure Thelma was telling me that she was going to let go and fly, and that I was to do the same. We were both going to be okay. I had been through a huge period of self-doubt. I had questioned my decisions about money, career, and a myriad of other things, all driven by fear. It seemed as if the little bird was mirroring exactly what I was feeling—fear. Just like the little bird, Thelma and I both had to get through our fears, and fly. Nature is one of God's favorite teachers.

Grief is a vehicle for transformation. When we have fully understood the extent of our loss, we can use that as a motivation for new life. We can choose to do something with what we've got left, whatever that might be. Transforming the loss involves placing the loss in the context of growth. I was looking at what I had left, and starting to add new threads and patterns to my quilt.

As upset as I had been about moving, it was the one factor that probably helped me the most. It clarified for me the scope of what I had left, and how I was using that to really start over. The move to a new house had actually helped me to accept my new identity. I was in a space that Tom had never lived in. It was as if the whole family was finally readjusting to being a family of four. The move pushed all of us to look at ourselves differently. I couldn't believe I bought a house all by myself. Wow!

In my ongoing assessment of what I had left, I realized I had been developing many skills over the past years at the agency that provided a perfect springboard for me into private practice. I loved doing therapy, and it seemed like a natural fit. Taking the risk to go into private practice was huge for me. I was fortunate to partner with someone who had an excellent reputation and was a seasoned veteran in the field. Therapists, by nature, are a pretty independent group. Private practice also gave me more control over my own time, which helped me to be more available for the children. Being able to work around my other priorities was becoming more and more important to me.

I was learning to rely increasingly on my Higher Power for guidance. We had been through two huge transitions in this year, our move and my new career. Each choice, each decision, led me to another level of awareness, whether it was a dating relationship or trying to decide whether to spend money on camp, vacation, or tuition. There was still a lot of loneliness in making these decisions alone, and not having someone sharing all those feelings and ideas. I was becoming aware of the various nontraditional ways information and answers would come to me. Following my intuition and being open to signs had led me to my new job and new home. When possible, I tried to include my children in my decision process. We were all a part of this journey together.

Raising my children alone was a constant challenge for me, especially a son. I was always questioning how I would handle this enormous job correctly. I wasn't a man and could not do all of the things with him or for him that a father would do, so how was he going to get the male relationship piece? My brother John was in Tulsa, so that was not an option. I proposed this question to my Higher Power not once, but many times. Well, again, an answer was provided, not according to the way I would have envisioned, but perfect for Tom Jr. at this difficult time.

Kelly had a great friend; his name was Mark. Mark became Tom's big brother and mentor. Mark was actually a lot like Kelly's dad. He loved sports, hunting, and fishing. I let Mark take Tom hunting and fishing at a young age. He coached Tom's little league team and was as attentive to him as a dad. Mark became the person Tom could rely on to have those little heart-to-heart talks. If I had a dilemma with Tom, I pulled Mark into the loop.

Mark always dropped in on Christmas morning. He knew we were up early. This particular Christmas, I heard a knock on the door, and knowing what was about to happen, let Tom open the door. I heard a little bell, gently jingling, and before I could get out of my chair, a precious, little ball of reddish-blond fur came wobbling into the living room, with Tom close at her heels. Everyone started yelling at once, saying how cute she was. That was the first time I met mandy, our golden retriever. Amidst arguing about who would hold her next, she engaged the entire family. Except to potty and sleep, her feet hardly hit the ground that day. I am sure mandy came to help me raise these children, especially Tom. In one way or another, she has become a best friend to all of them. Animals have a way of pulling love and humor into many difficult situations. We needed mandy. Mark gave us a special long-term gift that Christmas.

I knew Mark was picked by God and Tom to play this important role in young Tom's life, and somehow Mark knew it too and stepped up to the plate. I had to be open to allow the relationship, and Mark had to be willing—not a small commitment. It was a big assignment, and we were both willing to follow through with God's plan. There could not have been a better substitute.

There were many other men in the form of fathers, coaches, and role models in Tom's life. Tom commented once that he felt so fortunate to have been able to get to know so many of his friends' fathers so well. Each one of them touched his life in a certain way. Not having a fixed idea of what a dad should be, he really appreciated the unique qualities they each possessed. These men could not have been more supportive to Tom, including him in many activities and not showing him pity, but sensitivity and respect. There were fathers he golfed with, and others he hunted and fished with, and even some who asked him to come along on father-son activities. Those men were really special, sharing their time with Tom as well as their own sons. They became vitally important in his growth process.

I knew that as the only parent in this family, I set the tone and modeled values and behavior that the children would carry with them for a lifetime. What an awesome responsibility! At times it felt completely overwhelming. I certainly wasn't perfect. Saintliness was not one of my natural qualities. I realized that they would have to learn from my mistakes as well as my good decisions. Being a parenting team of one, there is no one else to help maintain a balance. How can children compare styles when there is only one parenting style? That promoted a lot of parent-child late-night talks, dialogue, and yelling. We were only human.

Because I was a therapist, I was often asked to give talks in the community. For my children it probably felt like being the minister's child—they were supposed to behave, and I was supposed to have all the answers. I recalled one talk on parenting that I had been asked to give at Kelly's high school on parenting. I was flattered. The assigned topic was children sneaking out and going to late-night parties. I felt very smug at the time and was so sure that Kelly had never done such a thing.

The night before I was supposed to give the talk, Kelly had several friends spend the night. One of the moms called my house to talk to her daughter. I went to wake her daughter up. As I pushed on what I thought was the girl, it felt soft. It was pillows! Lots of pillows stuffed in the bed and no girls. I couldn't believe it! I waited up for the girls to get home. It was a night I will never forget!

My talk the next night for the parents at her high school was entirely different than it would have been had that not happened. I knew I would never say never again. I was always learning in one way or another!

The saying that "it takes a village to raise a child" is very close to the truth. I was realizing more and more that without a partner to help me raise my children, support was an essential piece. This understanding drove many of my decisions regarding their involvement in schools, camp, and other activities. My children were certainly not going to listen to just me. Besides school and camp, these support systems also came in various forms, such as other parents, my daughter's friend Mark, and the families and friends we were close to. Two of the more important villages were both of the neighborhoods we lived in. Both of the homes we lived in were in old-fashioned neighborhoods, where neighbors were like best friends, and the children would play together everyday. As the children got older, I knew peer pressure would be an important factor in their beliefs and behaviors as well. The parents of my children's friends were an incredible support system and became an essential part of my village.

As I thought back over the years, I realized that the villages for my children were put into place shortly after Tom's death, and they changed with the years as the children grew older. The camp my children attended was one of the first villages that became part of this awareness. It was nestled in the beautiful hill country near Kerrville, Texas. Children who attended the camp rode on big buses that left from a church parking lot near our home. On a hot, July morning, I watched as the counselors loaded the big Greyhound bus with sleeping bags, pillows, laundry bags, and trunks with writing all over them.

Melissa was really excited. It was her first time away from home. She was only eight at the time, and I wondered if she would be able to separate from me. Sometimes children with only one parent tend to be clingy and have difficulty separating from their surviving parent. Melissa was my very precocious and independent child who nonetheless insisted on sitting in my lap at every available opportunity. It was her turn to get on the bus. She jumped up and gave me one of those wonderful hugs that almost breaks your neck and a big kiss on the cheek and ran through the doors of the bus with her best friend, Nancy. I had lots of salty tears that day. Parent moments never seem to stop! She never missed a summer of camp from that point on. Camp was an important part of the village, which continued through high school.

This was not just any camp. It is a wonderful, spiritual

place that supported and reinforced the values that I was trying to teach them at home. My children could go there and completely be themselves. In fact, one of the primary goals of the camp was for the child just to be himself or herself. There was no performance criteria involved. With all of the competition in school, this particular camp was a welcome change. It got them away from the city and into the heart of nature. Through the years, the children have reflected on what a grounding experience camp provided for them and the difference it made in their lives.

One year at camp, after Melissa was older, she had to give a talk pertaining to the most difficult thing she had to overcome in her life. She talked about the death of her father, whom she barely knew. She had to give this talk to a large group at a campfire called Round-up. She told me about the talk after she returned home. I am sure there was not a dry eye around the fire. Children need to talk about their losses. Although it had been many years since her father's death, she had never really talked about this loss in front of others, especially her peers, cementing it as a part of her identity.

I always picked the children up after the camp sessions, rather than having them ride the bus home. There is something about being in the Texas Hill Country and surrounded by nature that opens you up. I was staying in a small, old motel in a town near the camp. I was worried about finances and some other big decisions that were facing me over the next few months. I had been having trouble sleeping, and thought that the quiet of the secluded motel might help me rest.

That night I had a very vivid dream. Tom came to me and told me that things would be okay. He gave me no specifics about how things would unfold; I just knew that I could trust what he said. He was very clear. I couldn't recall many parts of the dream, except he seemed so real to me that I felt I could touch him. He was smiling and assuring me it would all be okay. And then I woke up. I had dreamed about Tom several times in the past, but this dream had a clarity the others lacked. Now he was clearly giving me information. I had felt like he was guiding me at certain times; I had signs, but no hard proof. I had asked for guidance recently regarding this big dilemma, but had not felt like I had gotten an answer, until now.

Realizing that Tom could communicate from the other side made death seem less daunting. Over the past few years, I had felt that I had been transforming my relationship with him from the physical to the spiritual. This dream was another piece of confirmation that the relationship with him had truly changed form. It was also difficult to talk about this transformative change with many people. Discussing death brings up fear—fear about what is on the other side, and fear that death is the end. I was realizing more and more that death is just the beginning of a transformation to another form.

Several mornings later, I was out hiking in an area near the camp. It was hot, and I had stopped and taken off my tennis shoes to rinse my feet in the clear, cold water of a creek. As I stepped into the creek, I heard a noise. I looked up. A deer had walked up at the same time and started to drink from the creek. As the deer stepped into the creek, I stood very still so I wouldn't scare him. We were both just standing there in that creek staring at each other, not an arm's length apart. He looked up, and our eyes locked in a gaze. He stared at me with his big, beautiful brown eyes, neither of us moving. He did not even seem afraid. I am sure we did not stand there for more than a minute, but it felt like an eternity. I was hardly breathing. I knew that if I moved, he would bolt. It was such a magical moment. It was as if we both knew we were supposed to be there in that moment, in that space, together. I watched him breathe; I breathed quietly, and then deeply, once again. All you could hear in the silence was our breath.

I do not think I understood the meaning of the word *oneness* until that moment. I had the stark realization that we are all divinely and uniquely connected by God's magnificent plan. The vision flashed in front of me. The deer, the cardinals, Thelma, Tom's last breath, me, my children—all a part of the same energy of creation, a greater universal plan that fits perfectly together, whether we are in the physical or spiritual form. That was also the special energy that filled my children each summer. What a gift!

The View from the Ridge

Looking back at the Valley

WE CAN EXPERIENCE TRANSFORMATION IN MANY WAYS. SOME PEOPLE CHOOSE IT, AND SOME ARE SIMPLY THRUST INTO IT BY EVENTS THAT CHALLENGE, EVEN THREATEN, OUR VERY EXISTENCE. I HAD BEEN THRUST INTO THIS UNKNOWN JOURNEY BY TOM'S UNTIMELY DEATH.

In John Schneider's book, *Finding My Way,* he talks about the three stages of grief: what is lost, what is left, and what is possible. It is difficult to move from one stage of grief to the next until we have a grasp on the one before it.

My one big loss, Tom, was very evident. I thought it was easy to see what I had lost. I did not initially recognize that my world was being dismantled, one step at a time. Grief comes off in layers, like peeling an onion. I had little conscious awareness of my constant sadness and disappointment, particularly during that first year, except when these losses seemed to present themselves to me, not once in a while, but every day. I would suddenly have a realization of seeing someone in the store who walked like Tom, or hearing a song that we both loved, or just realizing that I had no idea of what a normal routine looked like anymore. The reality that I had lost the ability to plan, and look forward to those next steps as couples do, forced me to change my thinking. The list went on and on. In the first year, it seemed as if the onion never stopped peeling.

Along with understanding what I had lost, it became necessary for me to explore what I had to let go of in order to move forward in my life. That seemed literally impossible. How can you move on to what is left if you don't know how to let go of the current thoughts, memories, and possessions? Determining exactly what to let go of, and what to keep, was confusing. That decision involves thoughts, ideas, material possessions, and an array of other pieces related to the loss. How do we let go of people and things that we love? It goes against our very nature. The reality is, in order to create the mental and physical space for something new to manifest itself in our life, we have to be willing to let go. Understandably, I grappled with that big, difficult question.

As I thought about letting go, I had to understand what letting go meant. Letting go does not mean I can never think about this person again. I realized that letting go does not mean forgetting, or blocking this person out of my mind, or even ceasing to stop loving this person. Memories are tricky things. We are desperately afraid that we will lose the memory, which makes us want to keep thinking about this particular person or thing. In fact, it is finding a way to hold on to the wonderful memories that allows us to finally let go. I was constantly afraid that I would forget what Tom looked like or his voice, or that the children would have no memory of him. I had to create ways to honor and hold on to those precious memories, so that I was sure they would always be there. Then and only then, could I give myself permission to let go.

Letting go means learning to love this person in a new way. As we transform our relationship with this person, it is important to have the right intention and thoughts regarding them while letting go. This person has been an important part of our life, and we would not be who we are if this person had not been in our life. They are part of our being. Even though we cannot love this person physically, we can send them love, through God. He knows and creates exactly what this person needs, whether they are here or have crossed over into the next life. Sometimes, if there is anger involved in a relationship, having the intention of sending this person love through God helps the healing process. It was an amazing experience for me to know that I could connect to Tom, and him love in a new way. I would not be who I am without the gift of this relationship, this person. His memory will always be carved in my heart.

In some cases, letting go can be a relief. Letting go is a process that we learn and relearn all of our lives. Nature is one of our greatest teachers. Everything in nature is a constant letting go, dying and coming back to life. As children, we learned to let go of toys and things that no longer fit. As we went through each year of education, we had to let go of certain beliefs, friends, and interests that no longer served us. As we grow and transform on our journey, we let go of paradigms that no longer work or fit into our lives. Letting go is a natural process. If we resist this natural process, we usually end up in some sort of turmoil and can't figure out why. I've been there, I've held on for dear life, and the relief when I finally let go was enormous! If we are to find and follow our thread, it is important to let go of things that hold us back or no longer serve us on our journey. The process of transformation is in the power of letting go.

Eventually we let go of everything in our lives—that

is death—and our soul moves into union with God. Watching Tom let go of everything suddenly put everything pertaining to life into a different perspective for me. He couldn't take anything with him, except his spirit. We had lots of stuff and he had to leave it all behind. We are just passing through. I realized that I was here to grow, change, discover my purpose, and work on my purpose to the best of my ability. I realized my purpose could have many dimensions and would change and unfold as I grew and changed. God uniquely designed this plan of letting go to help us release our attachments and rely on him.

The next challenge was looking at what was left. Sometimes that is the hardest part. We are so angry we don't even want to acknowledge what is left, because then we have to figure out what to do with it, and we have to change. And, no one likes change. On the surface, it looked like everything had been taken. I had no choice but to turn within and acknowledge the resources within myself. Piece by piece, God had helped me make the connections to understand the new threads that he would help me weave, to create the new pattern. Then—and only then—could I clearly define what was important enough to take with me on this new path. I was defining and reformulating my beliefs and values according to my standards, not ones that had been set for me by others. I felt like I was finally beginning to see what was possible, out of what I had left.

Grief leaves no part of us untouched. Every layer of our physical, emotional, and spiritual being is reformulated. I see the events, circumstances, and personal relationships in my life in a completely different way than I did years ago. In fact, nothing in my world is the same.

I have come to understand that grief is like a spiral. The stages go up and down, but it is never really finished. One layer seems to be complete, and something happens to bring more emotions bubbling to the surface. It is hard to even imagine the person I was when I was married to Tom. Today, I go for long periods of time and do not think about my losses. In fact, my losses look different to me now. I feel like I had been called upon to use every part of myself on this journey. My weaknesses, and the areas that I need to stretch and grow, are as clearly evident as my strengths. At times it feels like they are screaming at me! The weaknesses are as much a part of who I am as my gifts. I am called to embrace them as well.

I am always reminding myself that no one crosses my path by mistake. I have realized that there are no coincidences. In my practice, I feel like I have been privileged to meet the most amazing people. These are ordinary people, just trying to do their best and figure things out. No one has ever walked into my office and said, "I'm going to try and do my worst." As a therapist, I meet people in a vulnerable state. I know they are raw and real. When our eyes meet, just like my encounter with the deer, I know again the feeling of oneness. It is an honor to make the journey with them.

After eight years of doing individual and group therapy, I was interested in broadening my base, using what I had learned in some new venues. It felt like the time was right. The private practice with Suzanne was booming. We had two contracts with the state, as well as insurance and private-pay clients. It had been a success and provided me with the income and flexibility I had envisioned. But, I was feeling pulled into a larger arena. I had presented seminars in the past and really enjoyed it. The idea of doing workshops and sharing what I had learned was exciting to me. The children were older, and the demands on my time with them had lessened. I was not letting go of my practice completely, just partially, to make room for a new venture.

I partnered with my accountant, Laura, and together we developed a workshop to offer in the community. Laura had a great sense of humor and brought the balance of humor to my more serious nature in our presentations.

Our workshop focused on finance, balance, vision, and goal setting. It covered the transitions in life and how to navigate those places. Finance can be a pretty dry subject, but Laura could talk about it in a way that was simple and direct, with a humorous twist. She always included the idea of "big hat, no cattle." Everybody loved that.

I also felt that the workshop held an important message for women. In our society, there seems to be a stigma attached to single women raising families. I realized that I had also bought into that myth. Since there are so many single women out there raising families, and many do such an incredible job, I wanted to do my part in changing that myth or stereotype.

In large companies, you hear strategic planners talk about "scenarios." Usually there are several scenarios that are considered based on the values and goals of that company. This works in one's personal life as well. Laura and I put these two components together and gave workshops in the community called "Women in Transition." Both of us had lived, survived, and ultimately learned and thrived from these transitions. It was energizing and fun to give these presentations.

Laura and I did the workshops for about a year, and the outgrowth of those workshops was a company called Millennium Success Consultants. The purpose of the company was to provide training and outsourcing solutions to human resource professionals in corporations. I felt like I finally had the time to invest in something that was my own creative venture. I had a lot of connections that helped to open doors for the company too.

The first year, Laura and I were both amazed at the opportunities that appeared. Doors just seemed to open. *Synchronicity* is defined by Jung as "the cubic centimeter of chance, the seemingly accidental meeting of two unrelated causal chains in a coincidental event which appears both highly improbable and highly significant." It made the term synchronicity real in my life.

I kept a small private practice but focused most of my time on marketing for the company. It seemed as though it was going to pay off. We had some large contracts. Website companies were growing at that time, and I was even contacted and hired by a coaching website in California. The company flew me to Santa Barbara and paid for all my expenses. I felt very important!
In that first year, the business looked productive and promising. We had submitted proposals to several large oil companies and had contracted work already in place at other companies. We were on a roll, or so it seemed.

I was meeting tons of new people. I was thriving and enjoying the marketing aspect of this new career. It seemed like a time of expansion in my life. Once again, I was using skills that were a stretch for me. I was also trusting that if this was not the direction I was supposed to pursue, my Higher Power would let me know.

During this time I helped start a women's breakfast group. The purpose of the group was to pull together women in business who had similar values to support each other. The format was to be a topic discussion that would benefit us in our personal as well as our business lives. The group started out meeting at church and moved to a local club. We met for breakfast two times a month, and still do. The women in the group come from diverse backgrounds and occupations and are a dynamic group, to say the least. I had several magazine articles published about me during this time as well. It seemed as if everything in my life was supporting this new adventure.

As we entered into the second year of the company, a radical shift started to occur as the economy slowed down. This big career risk, much like death, was affected by forces that were completely out of my control. The large companies that had solicited our services were no longer outsourcing. Many of the smaller companies we worked with were going under. Things were not working out as well as we had projected. Laura and I were both disappointed and disillusioned. I had taken a risk with my career, and it did not work out. Once again, I could not understand where I was being led. Why did it seem I was going to go through another series of very difficult lessons related to this business? The financial implications were huge as well. My finances, which had been very stable for a long period of time, were strongly affected by this downward business spiral.

I did not realize it at the time, but I had completely relinquished my own power to this company and to my ego, which had become synonymous with the company. I had developed a pattern of always being focused in the future, not in the present. The present was getting harder and harder to focus on because the business was drying up.

It had seemed so easy in the beginning to rely on my own power to keep this company going. Later, I had to come to the realization that there is something very wrong when we feel we are indispensable, or that we are doing something totally on our own steam. It was as if I was making the company and my ego my sole focus and my center, not my Higher Power. Success can be very limited if we rely solely on ourselves.

I had lost sight of where true power comes from, and that is the center that is connected to our Higher Power. My creative center had been tapped into, but it was being used for the ego, not for a greater purpose.

There are a lot of things I know in theory, but until I integrate something into my life, I do not understand it. It's like eating chocolate cake. Once I know what the taste is like I never forget. I had read many things about the ego. Until this experience, I had not understood its power. I was a therapist, a spiritual therapist. I thought my center was based on God. I didn't really realize when my center shifted away from God to the company. The shift was so subtle that I didn't even know that it had happened until things started coming apart, and I was forced to pay attention. Huge contracts that we had worked on for months, and that were in the final stages, were being dropped. I couldn't understand it. I was learning a huge lesson in discernment and ego.

Understanding discernment was another big lesson for me. Discernment has to do with understanding the pulls of the ego, which tend to present themselves in the form of illusion. Illusion is a negative force, which masks what is real. Illusion that is directly tied to the ego is constantly seeking reassurance. The ego relates to the external, and that is exactly were my ego had taken me. The ego loves to be flattered and will do anything to stay in that position. Typically, the ego generates a fear mentality to help keep itself in place. The ego wants control, and fear is a great way to keep people from threatening the ego.

I have found that when a lesson is presented, it tends to show up in more than one area of my life. Discernment issues were popping up everywhere. I had met a lot of new people in my marketing position. I had a lot of contacts and could use them easily in connection with the business. I realized that while doors would open easily, there were several people who I had trusted who really just wanted to use my friendship for my contacts. As naïve as that sounds, it was something that had never happened to me. Trying to discern who really valued my friendship, and who was just flattering my ego, became an important part of this lesson for me.

We probably learn more from our failures than we do from our successes. I had learned a lot from the years we had run the company, and it was time for reevaluation. I also knew I had to find my center again.

The purpose of that difficult time in my life has continued to reveal itself. The years were not wasted. Starting the company allowed me the opportunity to explore other things that I had never had time for during the years I had such a large private practice. I am fortunate that I have been able to use my career in many different ways. I have done a lot of presenting and writing and have always maintained my private practice. The breakfast group was thriving and had introduced me to many women in my professional life with whom I have developed some close and wonderful friendships.

Other areas of my life had expanded during that year as well. I had always wanted to practice yoga. Maggie, a therapist friend, insisted I meet her at the class. When I entered the room, most of the people were lying down on their mats and towels with their eyes closed, being very still, quiet, and peaceful. I wondered if yoga was going to be energizing enough for me. The man leading the class looked very muscular and flexible. He nodded to me as I sat down on my towel, welcoming me to the class. It was quiet and no one spoke. I tried to position myself like everyone else so I wouldn't look out of place. The people in the class were all different ages and nationalities. Some were very old, and some were my age, and some were very young.

Two men started chanting, and everyone started chanting with them. I didn't know the words. It was similar to being in church and not knowing the songs, except you have on less clothes, and you sit very close to the person next to you. After the chanting, the man leading the class told us we were going to begin with breathing. I thought I knew how to do that, but I was wrong. This was not just regular breathing! It was a big-deep breath that felt like it was reaching down to my toes. Then we began the various yoga positions. I was stretching every part of myself. There were several positions I simply could not begin to master. I was practically falling down. As I looked around, I was shocked to see the older people in the class doing these positions with the agility of a twenty-year-old person. At that moment, I knew that I wanted to be just like them. I was determined to start a practice and master what I had seen that night. I was hooked! I attended that yoga class for some time. I learned that there are many types of yoga. In addition to walking and running, yoga is now one of the more important parts of my life and has enriched it on a daily basis. Yoga was leading me inward again, and back to balance.

I compared this time in my life to someone who had been pulled into a winding maze and couldn't find the way out. Upon leaving the maze, an enormous clarity seemed to emerge. I felt like I had been through some huge test and passed. I felt like I had made it through another dark night. But, I had navigated this dark night differently.

I knew I would get through. I knew the feeling; I had been on this path before. Now I had to remain open to what the next step would be and watch for the signs that would guide me there. I also needed to heal.

Finding the Waterfall

I WAS TRYING TO TRUST MY INTUITION AGAIN. A WOMAN'S NAME KEPT RESOUNDING IN MY MIND. I DIDN'T KNOW HER VERY WELL, BUT WE HAD WORKED TOGETHER WITH SEVERAL CLIENTS, AND I KNEW SHE WAS CONNECTED. IT COULDN'T HURT TO CALL. I WAS PRETTY FRAGILE AFTER THE EVENTS OF THE PAST TWO YEARS, STARTING AND RUNNING A COMPANY THAT DID NOT SUCCEED THE WAY THAT I HAD ENVISIONED. I PICKED UP THE PHONE ON THAT HOT, AUGUST DAY AND MADE THE CALL. ASKING FOR ADVICE WAS NOT SOMETHING THAT CAME EASILY TO ME. I KNEW THAT I WANTED TO FIND A POSITION IN THE NONPROFIT WORLD, IF POSSIBLE, THAT WOULD ALLOW ME TO KEEP MY SMALL PRACTICE AND WORK AT ANOTHER INSTITUTION PART TIME. I HAD NO IDEA THAT BY THE NEXT DAY, I WOULD HAVE A JOB OFFER.

My intention had only been to ask Mary for advice and direction. When I got through to her and told her the type of job I was looking for, she informed me that they had a position opening up at the place where she was working. In fact, she wanted me to come in and interview that day if possible! I couldn't believe it. The fit was almost too perfect. It was a children's grief center.

The director of programs was someone whom I had known of for several years. She was leaving the position in a few months. I had the exact experience that the center was looking for in that position. It couldn't have been a better fit. It felt like my center and intuition were connecting again. That was also my first experience with the higher agenda that goes on at a grief center.

One of the first evenings that I was at the grief center, one of the people on the board had stayed to visit. It turned out that he was the cousin of the family that had employed Tom at the time of his death. Several other people I knew were on the board of this nonprofit. I was starting to reconnect with a lot of people from my past—people whom I had known when Tom and I had been married. I know there are no coincidences. My circle was winding back to the center.

I would tell all of the new people who came to the grief

center, whether they were volunteers, interns, employees or clients, that they had something to heal, or they would not have been there. I had something to heal when I walked through that door. I did not have such an awareness then, but I know it now. The grief center is a healing place.

At the grief center, I had a lot of duties as director of programs, but one of my favorites was watching the families on a group night at the end of the evening. The families and volunteers all gathered in the living room together and sang this simple song, "Lean on Me." As I glanced around the room, I could see all races and classes, and as our eyes connected, I recognized the feeling. It is the oneness that transcends age, race, or religion. It is the same feeling I experienced with the deer at the creek and with my clients in private practice. I felt it again, here at the grief center. I knew what they were experiencing. I knew the pain. I also knew the hope that can follow the pain. I knew that they had the capacity to heal, even though they may not have known it yet.

I do a lot of public speaking. After I came to the grief center, one of my first talks was at M. D. Anderson. As I walked through the door, I was thinking about my last visit, when I was there with Tom, and the sadness that had engulfed me at that time. When I stood up to introduce myself, I smiled and began my story. I was back at M. D. Anderson for a different reason. I was there to educate social workers and medical staff about the grief process. "I have a lot to share." I stopped by Alice's office, the nun who was so much a part of our daily existence for the year Tom was ill. Her office was still filled with statues and pictures of angels from the many "Toms" in her life. The circle was winding back, once again.

One of my favorite quotations from Karlfried Graf Druchkeim is, "When you're on a journey and the end keeps getting further and further away, then you realize that the real end is the journey." In Jung's books, he speaks of a "mandala," which is the Sanskrit word for circle. When composing a mandala, you are trying to coordinate your personal circle with the universal circle. Making a mandala is a discipline for pulling all of those scattered aspects of your life and journey together. It's a way to identify your thread. I knew the time had come for me to work on my mandala.

It was my birthday. My birthday is one of those days when I look back on my life and really think about all the pieces and what is important. For me, it is a time for taking stock and, like the mandala, pulling all the pieces together into a new design. This day was no different, until late on Sunday evening.

I had talked with Tom Jr., who was away at college, early in the day. The phone rang about 6:30 in the evening and it was Tom again, only this time, he was very upset, and sounded like he was crying. "Mom, you cannot believe what is happening!" he said. "My house is burning to the ground! Everything I own, or have ever owned, is on fire! It is all gone! What am I going to do?" By now he was sobbing. I was twelve hours away by car. I was stunned and felt completely hopeless. There is absolutely nothing worse than being separated from your child when they are sobbing and hurting, no matter what their age. It was all I could do to ask him if he was all right, and if the other boys who lived in the house were okay. It turned out that they were all fine, no one was hurt.

He went on to tell me that he was standing in front of his house in Oxford, Mississippi, and that it was burning to the ground. A tree outside of the house had been hit by lightning and then fell on a gas line, which exploded in the kitchen. He and his roommates were in the room next to the kitchen, and had just left the kitchen moments before, after cooking dinner. They ran to the front door and barely got out alive. Now he was watching as everything he owned burned to the ground. His car, a Bronco, which was sitting next to the house, proceeded to explode into flames. He was devastated as he stood helplessly in the street, watching everything disintegrate before his eyes.

"Mom, I had grandma Thelma's poker table, and Dad's guitar, and his guns. My clothes ... I don't even have a pair of socks!" It was overwhelming. I was on the phone with him most of the evening. He had taken most of his worldly goods to school with him. His fishing and hunting equipment, his golf clubs, even his dad's guitar, which he had recently started playing, had all been burned beyond recognition. Gone. All gone. It was a miracle they got out alive.

The next day, Tom and his friends went back to sift through the rubble. As he sifted through the piles of ashes, he found three things, lying close together, that had not been destroyed: his Jesuit cross, a tin box of family pictures, and his checkbook. That was it; that was all that was spared. He said that it gave him chills when he found them.

Tom heard the message loud and clear. It was as if God had spoken directly to him. These were the three things that he would need to get thorough life: God, his family, and the ability to provide for himself. All of his exterior possessions had been destroyed. The message was different yet familiar; he was now to rely on his internal compass and the resources he had been given. The message in the fire made more of an impression on him than anything I could have taught him. It was by far the greatest gift I have ever received on my birthday—the gift of my son's life.

It was a close call, too close. Once again, I was reminded about how short the time is that we are here, and the fragility of life. I was also aware, once again, that I was not raising my children alone. Someone else was in charge. It was part of my circle, brushing with death again, and realizing anew the importance of each day of our journey.

When Tom Jr. came home, a few months after the fire, he went straight to my desk where I had kept a few of big Tom's personal possessions. He opened the desk and took out his father's wallet. He said, "Mom, it's time for me to have this. Mine was burnt up in the fire, and I want to use Dad's wallet. It's time for me to have it." Parent moments. As I wiped a few salty tears from my face, once again, I was reminded of the circle.

I am observing my mandala. My circle winds back to the beginning as I intertwine with each family I meet at the grief center. Working at the grief center pulled all the pieces of my journey together, both personally and professionally. God wastes nothing as he unfolds the greater plan. The pieces of my journey are carefully crafted together—Tom's death, my career as a therapist, the business training, and presentation skills—so carefully woven to fit perfectly into this new pattern.

Following the years at the grief center, I have moved back into private practice. Again, I am observing the rhythm of the pieces of my life as they connect in the most interesting pattern. I can now watch with anticipation and amazement as these pieces slide perfectly into place. Full circle. I always wanted to see the blueprint ahead of time, but that is no longer necessary. I am learning to say yes to God's plan and to trust. I don't resist as much anymore.

I agreed to give a talk at the grief center on "The Myth of the Happy Holidays." In digging through some of my old mementoes for something to inspire me, I came across the old newspaper article that had been published on my family the year Tom died. At the end of the article I was quoted as saying, "But you do get to start over. It won't be the same kind of life that Tom and I would have had, but it can still be a good life. I realize that the next twenty years will be pretty much what I make it."

It has been exactly twenty years since Tom died, and I did not have the blueprint ahead of time. How did I know that I would raise a family, and that the journey would be "what I made it"? Now I understand, as I pull out my mementoes from so long ago. The journey is part of the mystery and the adventure. And a plan that requires the answer, yes, and acceptance.

Loss is an underlying theme in everyone's life. Whether it is a loss from a relationship, death, family, job, possessions, or location, loss ignites the grief process in varying degrees. Our society as a whole does not want to look at the process of grief. It is painful and messy.

The word *dead* is practically taboo in our society. We have been forced to look at death in the face over the past few years. As a nation, and in the world, death is all around us. The events of 9/11, the world situation, and natural disasters have brought it to the forefront. Coincidence? I don't think so. How we think about death has a great impact on how we live our lives and what values we will choose to embrace.

While I was at the grief center, we did some training with medical interns to help them get in touch with their beliefs about death. After all, they were going to deal with it daily. Actually, we all deal with it daily. The exercise we did with them was to have them draw their concept of death. There is no right or wrong, just a concept. Have you ever drawn your concept of death? Use crayons and a blank piece of manila paper. It is an amazing experience. It puts you in the image, right there. It is very enlightening. It brings lots of tears. It was interesting to watch the results of those drawings. Death transcends all religions and beliefs, again, back to oneness. The individuals without any faith had a question mark or a blank paper, and a blank face, no emotion. That was sad.

Embracing grief requires us to understand the loss, and to integrate the experience into our being. We would not be who we are without the loss. As we reformulate loss, it can bring us to new levels of loving and living, and to new places within ourself and with others.

During the last few years, I have asked myself, "Could I have realized this any sooner?" No, not all at once. It has been a process. Each step of the journey has been like a piece of a puzzle that unfolds a little at a time. In fact, if someone had said to me right after Tom died or at any time during those first few years, that grief was a gift, it would have sent me over the edge. I am sure I never would have spoken to them again.

Grief has been my vehicle for transformation. Before my grief experience, I only knew God from a distance. Now I have a relationship with him. He is like my best friend. I know that if I stay connected to him in my center, the interior, he can provide all I need for the exterior. My relationship with Tom has transformed as well. He and I have a spiritual relationship, and I can call on him whenever I feel the need to do so. He makes his presence known in the most interesting ways and appears to be much wiser since he has transitioned to the other side.

My journey has not been easy, but is anyone's? Has it been happy and interesting and pretty amazing in lots of ways? The answer is yes, a lot of the time. Has there been sadness? Yes. Has it been scary? Yes. Has there been joy? Yes. Again I am reminded of the saying, "If God brings you to it, he will bring you through it." He has kept his end of the bargain, and I have tried to keep mine.

Oneness

AS THE SILVER TIP OF THE PLANE'S WING DIPPED SHARPLY TO THE SIDE, I FELT THE PIT OF MY STOMACH SWIRLING AS I LOOKED OUT THE WINDOW AND SAW THE ROUGH, GRAY ROCK ON THE SIDE OF THE MOUNTAIN. "HOW IS THE PILOT EVER GOING TO LAND ON THIS NARROW PIECE OF ROCK?" I THOUGHT TO MYSELF. "I AM SURE HE HAS DONE THIS BEFORE." I TIGHTLY GRIPPED THE SIDE OF MY SEAT AS I FELT THE THUMP OF THE WHEELS WHEN THE PLANE SLIGHTLY TOUCHED DOWN ON THE RUNWAY BELOW US. I STEPPED OUT OF THE PLANE AND INHALED; A DEEP BREATH OF MISTY, COOL AIR GREETED ME. I WAS GLAD TO BE IN COLORADO AND AWAY FROM MY HUMID HOUSTON. EVEN IF IT WAS ONLY A WEEK, I KNEW IT WOULD BE A TIME TO BE IN THE OUTDOORS AND EXPERIENCE THE ONENESS THAT HAD BECOME SUCH AN ESSENTIAL PART OF MY LIFE. THE TRIP TO COLORADO WAS AN EXPERIMENT OF GOING INTO THE UNKNOWN. WE HAD NO AGENDA OR CRITERIA EXCEPT TO BE OUTDOORS AS MUCH AS POSSIBLE.

I spotted his dark blue jacket hanging from his lanky frame as I stepped into the cool air and made my way up the runway to the doors of the terminal. I knew he would be on time. His grin broke into a big smile as he spotted me coming through the metal doors. He mirrored my excitement and anticipation about sharing this adventure. As I walked toward him, he greeted me with a big hug and lifted me off the ground. We did not have to wait long for my bag, and we made the short walk to his white truck, which was parked close by. He threw my bag in the back and helped me into the passenger seat. His brown eyes were dancing as he said, "You won't believe this town, it is so neat. There is so much I want to show you! You won't need anything but jeans and a jacket."

I had met Ron through mutual friends. He had spent many summers in Colorado as a child. He loved the outdoors and knew his way around the mountains. I knew I was in good hands. We had a lot in common, not the least of which was our love of the outdoors and a sense of adventure.

It felt like we couldn't waste a minute of this precious time. The next day, we headed out for our first hike, equipped with backpacks, rain gear, and drinking water. The soft, misting rain sweeping over the mountaintops dampened my skin as we started to make our climb up the narrow, bumpy road on the side of the mountain. I tipped my head back and let my eyes rest on the magnificent landscape and waterfall before me. The waterfall, cascading down from a higher elevation on the mountain, was our destination. I wondered if the path we were taking even went that high. There were a few other climbers who started with us, but decided to stop at various points along the way. A few brave, four-wheel drive vehicles passed us, but soon, there was no one else. The sheer size of the mountain at twelve thousand feet seemed daunting. Several hours passed as we stopped many times to catch our breath, not believing that after all the exercise we did on a regular basis, we were still apparently out of shape. I had to keep reminding myself that the walk was just like my life, one step at a time.

We finally got to the majestic, cascading waterfall, which, from the bottom of the mountain, had seemed so small in the distance. Now, at a closer glance, it was enormous as it erupted out of the side of the mountain. This powerful force of nature seemed as if it owned the mountain, its pounding forces throwing water on the rocks in front of us. The waterfall seemed to dare us to come closer. We felt the icy mist on our faces and bodies, leaving us wet with its force. It was to be looked at, admired, and listened to, this beautiful work of nature. I closed my eyes and listened to the relentless, powerful pounding. I felt the forceful rhythm surge through my body as I walked closer to the rocks at the waterfall's base. God designed nature to teach us: amazing gifts, if we can take the time to listen. I felt immersed in the embrace of its oneness, power, and strength. We had finally reached Bridal Falls.

Walking is fun, but sometimes riding can get you to places you would never see on foot. And, in our case, that also meant not having to catch our breath every few minutes. The next afternoon, we rented a blue, four-wheel-drive Jeep and headed for the dusty, rocky trails that circled in and out of the mountains. Well-stocked with water, we headed into the mountain range at dusk, just before the sun was casting its last beautiful rays of the day. As we wound around on the narrow, dusty trail, the sun was spray-painting vivid, brilliant orange, yellow, and silver colors on the sides of the mountains for all to see.

As we were winding deeper into the range, we came to the top of a ridge, and the site that opened before us made us catch our breaths. The Jeep came to an abrupt halt, and we just stared, not speaking. Ron asked in a shocked voice, "Do you see what I am seeing?" Out of nowhere, a lush, green, open valley appeared before us, with what looked like hundreds of sheep in a herd. The sheep stood very still, cascading over the pasture and ridge of the rolling valley, quietly nibbling at the lush grass. Some of the sheep were white, and some had precious black faces—innocent, untouched, and peaceful. Watching from a small hill near us, a sheepherder stood tall and erect, with a staff in his hand. In the middle of the herd was a small, frozen pond, upon which two large white sheep dogs lay, keeping a steady gaze on us, the new arrivals. As if in slow motion, the sheepherder raised his staff, and nodded at us. Nothing else moved, lest something might disturb this eloquent balance.

It was as if we had stepped into a scene from a biblical painting, the exquisite rays of the sun bouncing off the sides of the valley, the lush green grass, the emerald blue sky, and the peaceful, still sheep, with their protectors, the dogs and the herder, watching over them. It did not seem real. If I had not had another person with me to validate that we were witnessing this perfect scene, I would have had to pinch myself. I felt like I was a part of this picture, this moment, and was overcome with emotion as tears started to run down my face. We sat there for some time, drinking this all in. The first thing that came to my mind was the Twenty-third Psalm, beginning with the words, "The Lord is my Shepherd."

It was God speaking in pictures, rather than words. What an amazing way to tell us that he was watching over us. It was a profound moment and gift. I shall carry the image in my heart forever. The scene reminded me of the many valleys that had been a part of my life, and how I was watched and protected. The message was consistent, oneness and nature, which speaks the language of our soul.

It had become clear for me that the journey of oneness with God is the goal of a lifetime. He created everything and everyone on this planet. Waking up to the possibilities of how this all works together is simply amazing. It seems that each of my lessons had become an opportunity to become more trusting and closer to him. No lesson is wasted, and there are no coincidences. We are all connected by the same life force. Oneness is the higher awareness of our connection to every living, breathing, plant, animal, or person. All the tools and opportunities have been placed in our paths to help us accomplish this task.

Once you have experienced the awareness of oneness in small portions, the experience seems to build. My experiences started out very small, and gradually increased with my own self-awareness. My experience of oneness began with Tom's last breath, as if I was breathing with him, and watching him take that last breath. It continued with the deer at the creek, the cardinals, my clients, the people at the grief center, certain types of prayer, meditation, yoga, certain types of music, and the list goes on and on. As I have become aware of the feeling of oneness, I realize it happens all the time. Being fully present to others is a way to experience oneness. As I continue to choose oneness, opportunities in my life seem to unfold in an endless way. It is a state of being that I choose to enter into. Meditation, going into the gap, is the form of prayer I use daily to go into a state of oneness with God. This is my breath, my lifeline, and he provides the rest.

I could hear the sound of the water as we climbed up the side of the mountain, carefully placing each foot on the soft, slushy mud and dirt, trying hard to grip the surface of the mountain with my hiking boots and not slip. It was our last day in Colorado, and we were hiking to a waterfall we had heard about that was not as large as the one on the first day and had no clearly marked trail. In fact, it had no trail at all! We were not sure where it was and felt like explorers, trying to find a hidden cave, as we navigated the rocky terrain.

When we passed the dribbling streams of water coming out of the rocks, we knew we were beginning to get closer. As the small streams became wider and merged into one, we were able to enter the flowing water and walk upstream toward the falls. We stopped and put on our waders, which provided warmth and dryness, and started walking through the icy water, trying hard not to slip on the uneven rocks. The closer we got, the louder the pounding sound became, so we knew it wasn't far. Our excitement was building; looking for this waterfall was like searching for hidden treasure.

Finally we saw it. The white sheets of water were tumbling out of the large rock formations at the top of the mountain. We continued to carefully navigate the slippery stream as we continued upward. Our heavy boots felt like lead. We sloshed toward the icy pool of water and slippery rocks as we came closer to the falls. It was like a magnet was drawing us, as our determined, deliberate steps brought us deeper into the frigid water near the base of the falls. We stopped and stood within a few feet of it, feeling the current pulling at our legs.

I was mesmerized by the kaleidoscope of color cast from the blue-green and pink rocks that sparkled through the clear streams of water as it cascaded into the pool surrounding us. I felt the spray of the icy mist on my arms and face. It felt like we were absorbing the force of its strength as the water came down in endless pellets around us. We stood at the base in the icy water for some time, mesmerized by the magical rhythm of this powerful waterfall. I knew few people had been privileged to witness this awesome sight. I felt small and unsteady as the force of the water pulled at me. Ron gently reached out and put his arms around me, and drew me close into his side to steady me in the swirling water. In the perfect quiet, all you could hear was the breath of me, the breath of Ron, and the steady, cleansing gush of the rhythm of the icy water, as it cascaded over the waterfall into the pool at our feet. Another transformative gift of oneness, from the power of creation.

If we are ever to give our gifts to the world, it has to come out of our own experiences, and not someone else's. The process of living is designed to get us in touch with our own soul and spirit. Recently I heard Deepak Chopra talk at a church near my home. He said, "Until we experience and enter the unknown, we cannot touch with the creative part of our self, which touches with our spirit and awakens our soul." Ron and I shared a lot on this unplanned trip into the unknown. At every turn, it seemed that our experiences were providing the backdrop for the consistent messages of the divine oneness that lives within each part of creation, and had been the constant theme of my life experience.

If we are ever to discover the intricate aspects of our own truth, we must be present and embrace each experience as it presents itself to us, whether that experience is positive or negative. The great question is, "What do I need to learn from this?" Every experience is presented to us as a tool for learning. Epicletus, the Greek sage, advised his students, "Learn to wish that everything should come to pass exactly as it does."

There has been a lot written in recent years about finding your purpose, and how to do that. I had that burning question as I embarked on this path. It is not everyone's question, but it was mine. Our purpose can reveal itself as we go deeper into our connection with oneness, which opens the portal to our soul, and enables us to discover the divine within ourselves. If we make a conscious decision and intention to find our purpose, the opportunities will start to appear in our path to support this search, leading us to discover the creative part of our being. I could have refused the call, I could have said no. If I had said no, I am sure my path would have been quite a different journey.

Grief was the vehicle that God put in my path to help

me transform physically, emotionally, and spiritually. Embarking on this interior journey opened me to the mystery and understanding of the divine oneness with all of life, which enabled me to listen to my soul and purpose. This was my amazing gift from grief.